THE PERFECT
FIRST
MATE

THE PERFECT
FIRST
MATE

A woman's guide
to recreational
boating

JOY SMITH

SHERIDAN HOUSE

First published 1999 by
Sheridan House Inc.
145 Palisade Street
Dobbs Ferry, NY 10522

Library of Congress Cataloging-in-Publication Data

Smith, Joy.
    The perfect first mate : a woman's guide to recreational boating / Joy Smith.
        p. cm.
    Includes index.
    ISBN 1-57409-083-6 (alk. paper)
    1. Boating for women. I. Title.

    GV777.57 .S55 1999
    797.1'082—dc21

                                                                99-049207

Illustrations by Mary Valencia
Text design by Jeremiah B. Lighter

Printed in the United States of America

ISBN 1-57409-083-6

For Gil,
the love of my life

ACKNOWLEDGEMENTS

Many thanks to all the wonderful people who helped make this book a reality: Lothar Simon and all the folks at Sheridan House; and Mary Valencia, who illustrated this book to perfection. I couldn't have done it without the thoughts and opinions of my dear friends and fellow boaters, Nancy Sheridan and Lisa Musumeci. Noreen Wise gave me the confidence to pursue writing, and Debbie Lacilla helped me grammatically. I especially thank my family—Gil, Meara, Lisa, and Richard—and all the rest of my family and friends for their support, and for listening to me babble about this for years.

THE OWL AND THE PUSSY-CAT

The Owl and the Pussy-cat went to sea
In a beautiful pea-green boat:
They took some honey, and plenty of
money,
Wrapped up in a five-pound note.
The Owl looked up to the stars above,
And sang to a small guitar,
"O lovely Pussy, O Pussy, my love,
What a beautiful Pussy you are,
You are,
You are!
What a beautiful Pussy you are!"

Pussy said to the Owl, "You elegant fowl,
How charmingly sweet you sing!
Oh! let us be married; too long we have
tarried;
But what shall we do for a ring?"
They sailed away, for a year and a day,
To the land where the bong-tree grows;
And there in a wood a Piggy-wig stood,
With a ring at the end of his nose,
His nose,
his nose,
With a ring at the end of his nose.

"Dear pig, are you willing to sell for one
shilling
Your ring?" Said the Piggy, "I will."
So they took it away, and were married
next day
By the Turkey who lives on the hill.
They dined on mince and slices of quince,
Which they ate with a runcible spoon;
And hand in hand, on the edge of the sand,
They danced by the light of the moon,
The moon,
The moon,
They danced by the light of of the moon.

EDWARD LEAR (1871)

Author's note: I used to recite this poem to my captain on long sails when things got boring. He preferred it to my singing.

Contents

Introduction

SO, YOU'VE BOUGHT A BOAT

You've been apprehensive since you brought home that first brochure, and now the launching is imminent. You've even spent a few restless nights wondering if you have the stamina to deal with all those hair-raising high-seas adventures you've been reading about. Visions of 10-foot waves and man-overboard emergencies dance through your head. And then you realize that the worst problem you'll have to cope with is Captain *My Way*.

He has been rubbing his hands with glee because the boat is finally going in the water. He's adventure bent. You're scared. He has more plans for you than you want. How on earth are you ever going to keep this boating thing under control? With all that boating stuff he's collecting, where are you going to fit your personal gear? How will you cope with doing without? How *does* one cope aboard a boat?

This book is your guide to managing all those pesky "first mate" tasks that you will most likely be responsible for, while at the same time keeping enjoyment in the forefront. Read it for fun, then read it for you. I've sailed in your boat shoes and have survived Captain *My Way*. And in the process, I have come to treasure my boat more than my home.

GETTING INTO THE SAIL OF IT

No matter how simple or luxurious your new boat is, it won't take you long to slip into the mindset of a seasoned boater. Your captain will think and talk about nothing but his boat to the point of embarrassment. Worse yet, you will catch yourself chiming in. Non-boater friends will start avoiding you. You'll hire a neighborhood kid to mow that lawn, which is quickly becoming a hayfield, so you can spend every spare minute cramped on a boat whose entire space is probably smaller than your kitchen at home. Perhaps it's the child in us that drives us into these cocoon-like cubbies where we feel cozy and content.

On our boats, we spend quality time with family and friends—we don't even miss television. Boating brings us back to the world. We struggle with an alcohol stove we feel fortunate to have and perk coffee over a burner the old-fashioned way. We watch a magnificent sunrise in our cockpit holding a mug of coffee that somehow tastes better than any coffee we've ever made at home. With every sip we savor the velvet tranquillity of the early morning water and the sea sounds of crowing gulls.

As boaters, we are exposed to the great outdoors, truly communing with the elements. Even if you have been a houseplant all your life, you'll glow in the warmth of the sun, thrive on the brush of the wind, and be invigorated by the splatter of raindrops. You'll inhale the fresh, salty air like you can't get enough. You will feel alive.

Listening to the ocean as we gaze across the water relaxes our bodies and clears our heads. The mundane things we were so worried about at home seem unimportant against the backdrop of waves that seem to expand our minds forever. We can sail all day yet converse about nothing relevant. We aren't bored. The hours fly.

When we aren't aboard, we're planning our next excursion. Our "condo on the sea" takes us to little islands and nestles us in undiscovered coves. Some of us relish the sport of boating, the heel of the sail, racing to win. Others are content to drop the anchor and fish, dive, or snorkel. Sometimes, we just bask in the sheer pleasure of hanging around the dock exchanging "boatspeak" with our buddies.

THE JOY OF SLOTH

The transition into the boating life seems like magic because it only gets better. We become joyously slovenly. Our captains tend not to shave, and develop the pinching, grisly look of a derelict we'd usually avoid. Routine skin cleansing seems like a needless chore as we flop onto our berth at night without even brushing our teeth. In the morning, the bra gets conveniently forgotten. We throw on a loose T-shirt and a pair of stretchy shorts, and consider ourselves dressed for the day. By the time we return to civilization, we need a long, hot soapy shower and a complete overhaul before daring to venture out in public. Isn't it grand?

The fresh salt air produces a yawn and gives us a hearty appetite. Before long, our pants are tight from adding a daily cocktail and hors d'oeuvres to our regular diets. The truth is, there is little exercise on a boat at rest other than raising the hand to the mouth. Snack foods are standard fare on a boat. Don't even try to diet until boating season is over.

There is a tendency, when at dock, to relax. We lie around the boat and read, sun ourselves, and then go below to take naps—all those wonderful little luxuries we feel too guilty to enjoy on a Saturday at home.

A BOAT IS A HOLE IN THE WATER
YOU PUT YOUR MONEY INTO

"Marinaland" is a world where it's quickly apparent that everything you need or want for your boat costs more than you care to spend. Your captain will haunt the marine stores looking for shackles, lines, fenders, and electronic toys while you fill the time in the galleyware and nautical clothing aisles.

We boater wives spend our winters surrounded by marine catalogs and making field trips to every boat show within driving distance from our homes. As novices, we sign up for every boating course we can manage and voraciously read every article and book about boating we can get our hands on. Discussions about the boat fill cold winter evenings with the warmth of anticipation.

Outfitting our boats becomes a winter hobby. Preseason evenings, we collaborate with our captains to make copious lists of nautical necessities, from computer software to stainless steel shackles. We order monogrammed towels, blankets, and fender covers and choose a marine dinnerware pattern. We stalk department stores searching for odd-sized storage containers and tiny rugs to fit the oddly shaped nooks of our new home.

The advent of spring brings a torrent of catalog deliveries to our doors. We pile box after box of new gizmos for our boats in our basements, garages, and wherever else they will fit. Each box brings us closer to the day we can finally end our long winter wait with the big splash.

By the end of the first year, your boat is apt to be better equipped than your home. In fact, by the time you are perfectly outfitted, it's likely you'll want a bigger boat and will have an excuse to begin shopping all over again. You and your captain will find yourselves whiling away time at boat shows, traveling near and far to traipse through booths and climb on and off boats you can't afford. Talk of the next boat borders on reality as you ooh and aah about what you don't have. You'll collect plastic bagfuls of literature that will languish by the TV chair or in the magazine basket in your bathroom. It's catching. Like with a new home, there always seems to be something you need or want.

THE INEVITABLE—BECOMING CIVILIZED ON A BOAT

As the seasons wear on, our tolerance for roughing it erodes to craving onboard luxuries. We dream of a flush toilet, pressurized hot and cold water, and a stove that actually bakes and broils. Visions of refrigeration dance before our eyes as we tote that same jar of mayonnaise back and forth all summer. If we don't have dockside power, we beg an alternative—an inverter, a generator, or whatever will allow us to plug in our hair dryer. All manners of electrical appliances creep into our storage bunkers—coffeepots, toasters, fry pans, microwave ovens, and heaters. They are all things we have to have, of course, in what has become our summer residence.

There is a little sadness in becoming civilized on a boat. We spend more time in that galley we've stupidly equipped with all the conveniences of our kitchens at home. We no longer have an excuse for boater's hair when we can shower, shampoo, and blow dry. We feel obligated to dress up a bit more if our lockers are roomy enough to hang our nice clothes and there is no excuse not to plug in an iron. It gets worse. Some boats are equipped with washers and dryers. And, instead of sitting in the cockpit enjoying the stars at night, we may have sunk so low as to have brought our television to the boat to watch *Seinfeld*.

But whether you are cruising on a 23-foot boat or a 60-foot

yacht, all that will matter to you is being on the water. You will learn to cope with the hairiest situation, then be elated when you do. For every exciting sailing moment, there is one of pure tranquility. There is so much to delight in as long as you and your crew are comfortable, safe, and well fed. You'll learn to plan, to pack, to organize, and to manage your boating activities for optimal enjoyment of the wonderful world of boating. It's a great ride. Don't be afraid of it. Get that boat loaded and go sailing!

PART ONE

You're in It
for the Long Haul

AND I DO MEAN HAUL! If you have ever done any camping, you'll know exactly what I mean. There's no way to duck hauling except to send your captain off early with a loaded car and connive to arrive empty-handed several hours later. But even then, you won't be able to avoid the tiresome work. All your gear will need to be stowed. So, the drill is this: everything must be crammed into your car, then carted to and stashed away on your boat.

Taking time to think through what gear to bring to your boat and how to get it there intact will save you last-minute hassles with storage and spills. Whether you are setting up your boat for the season or for a short vacation, the task can be frustrating. Most often, all those little tidbits you decided are essential to bring on board typically amount to a heap bigger than the trunk of your car—and maybe even bigger than your boat! Don't despair. Planning and packing get easier with practice. You will become so organized that you'll have what you need when you need it and you'll even manage to find places for *your* necessities. Think about the size of each item you're hauling to the boat. If it's too big to carry, it probably won't fit in your boat—so leave it home. You will come to define your needs and learn you can manage nicely without TVs, VCRs, and evening gowns.

CHAPTER

1

Packing It In

CHOOSING THE RIGHT GEAR FOR THE RIGHT JOB

Begin by using the right gear. Gather up any of these items you have on hand: duffel bags, waterproof toiletry bags, fanny packs, sturdy canvas tote bags, plastic and net bags, and portable coolers.

Dust them off and check them for fitness. You can replace and add to your collection as you get into the routine of packing and schlepping. By choosing a container up to the task, your gear will arrive at its destination without dripping, scattering, or getting broken.

Personal Gear

Let's start with the easy part—packing your clothes and personal belongings. Leave your standard rectangular leather and nylon suitcases in the closet at home. Square corners, even soft ones, don't work well in the curvy confines of a boat. Suitcases are clumsy to maneuver, awkward to stow, and frustrating to live out of. Try it some weekend and you will see what I mean. Instead, opt for water-resistant or waterproof duffel bags. They are pliable, scrunchable, stackable, and abusable. Whenever I invite guests for an overnight stay, I caution them to bring duffels instead of suitcases. You'll find a huge assortment of styles in marine catalogs, at boat shows, in traditional stores, or in catalogs from Eddie Bauer, Lands' End, and L.L. Bean.

Corralling grooming aids into waterproof or rubber-lined toiletry cases keeps them dry, neat, and accessible. Sturdy bags with easy-to-grab handles that hang in the shower or on a clothes hook make life easier when there is no dry surface in the marine head or shower to set down your toiletries. Keep your bag organized by choosing a style that allows you to easily grab your shampoo and soap. Some bags even have removable mesh inserts that can be hung right onto the showerhead.

For items you need to keep at your fingertips, fanny packs are indispensable. They are useful for keeping things as precious as your boat keys, house keys, car keys, and glasses, from dropping overboard or into the bilge. And, fanny packs are lightweight, water resistant, and allow you to move and travel with your hands free.

Canvas Totes

I have been told that canvas totes were originally called ice bags. While charter cruising in the Grenadines, we stopped to buy ice. Instead of the five-pound plastic bags we were accustomed to in the States, we could only find loose cubes—which is when we tested the concept that canvas will hold water. The dock attendant filled our tote with 10 pounds of cubes and we went off chuckling in our dinghy, armed with the means to chill many rounds of cocktails.

Peruse any marina and you'll notice one commonality among boaters—they use canvas totes for carrying almost anything from tools to food supplies. And for good reason. Canvas totes are waterproof and support a tremendous amount of weight without ripping. Avoid packing provisions in paper bags. They are useless when wet and will never survive the heavy loads you'll be trucking to your boat. When we first started boating, what did I know? Plastic bags were barely invented back then. I took all my groceries to the boat in the paper bags the store packed them in. Not only were the packages unwieldy to handle, but the bottoms got wet when we tucked them in our dinghy for the ride to our mooring. What a mess! The eggs broke, the fruit bruised, and the rolls looked like someone sat on them.

Sturdy totes of all sizes, colors, and styles can be inexpensively purchased at your friendly marine store, at boat shows, or through boating catalogs; most cost less than $20. These all-purpose totes can survive the rigors and splashes of a dinghy ride and will not break even when loaded with several six-packs of soda. Look for durability—a double canvas bottom and double sewn straps. Then pray that the dye won't run onto your deck when the bottom of the bag gets wet. The longer-handled styles are nice because you can sling the bags over your shoulders, leaving your hands free to carry—what else—more bags. Zippered bags are convenient for securing the contents, although my bags are usually so full I often can't pull the zipper shut. A front zipper or pocket is handy for keeping keys, cash, and other small items separate. Smaller totes work well for heavier items, such as cans and bottles, and you won't be tempted to overfill them. Set aside a few nice-looking medium-sized bags to remain on the boat and use these as going-to-the-shower totes or beach bags.

> SHE SAID: *"What's this black gooey stuff in this bag?"*
> HE SAID: *"Leave that alone, it's the oil pump for the boat."*

I also advise squirreling away a few clean totes for your food and kitchen supplies. Once the captain has commandeered a tote for his engine maintenance gear and tools, the bag is a goner. The filth and grease that stain these totes' interiors render them unsavory for food or clothes. If any of your canvas totes get damp, be sure you allow them to dry in the sun before folding them away. Attack fresh mold spots with a spray of an all-purpose mildew remover that's safe for canvas. Set-in mold spots and grime don't launder well. If you try to bleach the stains, the colors will fade and the bags will lose their stiffness.

After several years of recycling canvas totes, you may want to invest in a top-of-the-line tote made of canvas that has been treated for added strength and durability. Expensive, but not fraught with the problems of traditional canvas, these bags can withstand years of exposure to sun and rain, resist mildew, and clean easily.

Indispensable Plastic Bags

> HE SAID: *"Shall I take this trash bag to the Dumpster?"*
> SHE SAID: *"No, take it to the car, it's our luggage."*

Plastic bags. What would we do without them? The uses for plastic bags on a boat are endless, so stock up on all sizes and shapes.

Transport lightweight, bulky items such as pillows, blankets, and PFDs (Personal Flotation Devices) to your boat in large, drawstring bags designed for trash. Handle ties on the bags make the load easy to secure and carry, and the plastic protects the goods from rain or splashes on your trek out to the boat. After you get aboard, store the gear in the same bags to protect it from the dampness and odors often found in closed lockers and cubbyholes.

Save empty plastic bags for trash. On those rainy days when everything is wet, there is no substitute for a plastic trash bag for dinghying your gear to shore and dashing to your car. Drop the packed canvas totes and duffels into large trash bags to keep them and their contents dry, then unload the bags from their plastic protectors right into your car. After you have gratefully changed into dry clothes, you can even shuck your foul-weather gear or wet clothes into these bags for their trip home to the clothes dryer.

When you purchase new blankets and linens, set aside the clear plastic, zippered bags that often encase them. These make great see-through, protective storage containers for linens and pillows. They are sturdier than trash bags and their square shape allows you to flatpack folded towels, sheets, and blankets. And, you don't have to dig through them to find out what's in them.

Recycle those pesky supermarket plastic bags that pile up in your drawers and closets at home by using them to keep groceries and small items grouped and easy to find when you pack and unpack them. Be a good environmentalist and vow never to discard them unless they are full of trash, recycled bottles and cans, or too riddled with holes to reuse. Purchase several sizes of sealable plastic bags, such as the zippered variety, and keep them on hand for airtight, moisture- and insect-resistant food storage of cereals, chips, lunch meat, and leftovers.

Net Bags

Net bags are cheap and there is a multitude of uses for them on a boat. They are available in nylon or cotton mesh; either will work for your storage purposes. Some have handles, others have drawstrings, but both work for anything from collecting and stowing small items to dirty clothes containment. The advantage of net bags over plastic is that they breathe and keep items well ventilated.

They are particularly good for transporting and storing wet or damp items, such as snorkel gear and wet bathing suits. I also use them to keep refrigerated foods that hold condensation, such as fruit, dry and fresh. Look for places to hang them up and out of the way in berths, an ice chest, or a locker. Net bags are only as heavy as their contents, they launder well, and they dry quickly.

Coolers

Hard coolers, soft coolers, Styrofoam coolers, or whatever type you have—you will need one or more of them. Coolers are some of the hardest working packing items you will use. If your boat doesn't have an ice chest or refrigerator, you'll most likely set up your cooler at home and place it intact on your boat for use during your stay. Otherwise, your cooler will function as a device to get your frozen and refrigerated foods to the boat without meltdown, or to keep food and beverages chilled for off-boat excursions.

Start by using whatever type of coolers you have on hand, then supplement those with sizes and shapes to meet your carting requirements. When considering size, remember to allow extra space for ice or ice packs. Storing unpacked coolers can be a problem where space is tight, so allocate a place to keep empty containers or take the extras back to your car once you've unpacked.

I am a great fan of soft coolers (and I don't mean the plastic type you buy at the pharmacy for school lunches), but it's surprising how few boaters have discovered them. I became a convert several years ago when I first saw soft, quilted cooler bags on display at a boat show booth. I admit I was attracted by all of the bright colors that were available (you can color coordinate with your boat decor). It's easy to overlook these most practical bags in stores or catalogs, so maybe that explains why many folks aren't aware they exist. Marine-grade, soft cooler bags cost a bit more than traditional hard coolers, yet years of usage have convinced me that they are the most practical choice for boaters. My original bag has faithfully withstood several years of abuse and still keeps food cold. I have since added several sizes to my supply.

Soft coolers keep food just as cold as hard coolers, but don't hurt when you bang your shins on them. Unlike hard coolers, they don't require two hands or two people to carry them (unless they're packed chock-full of ice and cans). You can often comfortably sling one over your shoulder, thereby freeing up both hands. Once on the boat, soft cooler bags can be unpacked and stowed flat just like boat bags, or you can continue to use them for beverages or food aboard. For your trip home, repack them with returning cold goods or clothes.

Soft coolers are less destructive than hard ones when under way. Keep them from dancing by securing their shoulder straps around a stationary, out-of-the-way spot below deck or in the cockpit. If you charter a boat, it is always nice to bring your own soft cooler. Pack it with clothes for traveling to and from your charter pickup point, then enjoy it as an ice chest while aboard.

PACKING SMART

A poorly packed load is harder to carry and deteriorates at the least opportune time. Developing a packing routine for trips to the boat will keep disasters to a minimum and make the task almost effortless.

Pack as You Shop

Begin the packing process by grabbing and assembling items you need to bring to the boat as you see or obtain them. Think before you haul. Is there an easier way to do this? If you include boat supplies on your weekly household shopping list, do you carry all the bags to your kitchen, sometimes climbing a flight or two of stairs, before sorting out the boat supplies, only to repack them and return them to your car? I learned the hard way that there are a couple of ways to tackle this beast.

Keep some spare totes and a cooler, preferably a soft style or one you can place in your refrigerator, in your car. On a hot day, you may wish to pre-chill the cooler with a few ice packs. In the store, drop boat supplies in either bag as you purchase them and put them into the car. For major supermarket excursions, try sorting your boat supplies from your groceries right at the checkout. Note I said *try*. Although this method is most efficient, it can only be accomplished if you are organized, persistent, and prepared to ignore the glares of all the people waiting in line behind you. Few checkout clerks are that tolerant, so you'll have to move fast. Or better, sort your groceries right from the cart in the supermarket parking lot, digging out boat supplies and placing them either in canvas totes or the cooler. Your remaining home-bound groceries may be a bit disordered but surely no worse off than they were before. If you won't be going to your boat soon, remove the cooler and place it unzipped or topless in your refrigerator until you are ready to leave.

Another packing option is to keep totes in your garage or just inside the entry door to your home and do your sorting in either place. Collect refrigerator goods going to the boat in supermarket plastic bags and refrigerate or freeze them until you're ready to leave. Unless you need the trunk space or will be changing cars, leave bulky items such as bags of charcoal and packs of soda right in your trunk. By your next trip to the boat, your supplies will be pretty much packed. Just add the last-minute things and toss the prepackaged frozen and refrigerated items into a cooler with ice packs or ice, and you're ready to go.

Use common sense. Balance the weight in your tote bags by distributing heavy items evenly among them. Use plastic bottles and cardboard boxes to separate glass bottles. Unless you're Hercules, don't put all the six-packs in the same bag. Stop while you can still lift the bag, because you probably will be stuck carrying it.

Protect Fragile Items

HE SAID: *"I've got the car loaded. Let's go."*

SHE SAID: *"Where'd you put the green canvas bag with the bread?"*

HE SAID: *"It's in there, somewhere."*

Loaves of bread and rolls will squash when you pick up the handles of your tote, so pack them loosely. Use a separate tote or place them on top of a square-loaded tote that's not likely to crush inward when you gather the handles to pick it up. Keep an eye on that bag with your soft goods when it goes into the car, making sure it's securely placed on top of your other supplies, or you'll be serving pancake sandwiches. Pita bread, which is flat, poses less of a handling problem. Bread is fragile. Treat it as if it were eggs.

Speaking of eggs, the best way to transport them, other than in their original carton, is in a plastic, latching egg holder that you can find at almost any camping or marine store. The eggs will be safe and secure and won't make a mess in your cooler or tote. For easily bruised vegetables or fruits, such as grapes, peaches, plums, and strawberries, separate them and store them in plastic containers. Although the containers take more storage room in your cooler or tote, the fruit will remain fresh and unaffected by a neighboring six-pack. Group non-delicate fruits and vegetables in plastic supermarket bags or net bags and place them near the top of your cooler or boat bag for the trip. Unpack the bags into your cooler or fruit bowl when you arrive. I find a tiered, hanging, wire mesh basket indispensable for keeping my fruits and vegetables off the counters and readily available.

Beverages are weighty. Opt for plastic bottles or aluminum cans. Some outdoor supply stores carry bottles and jars that are advertised to be leakproof, but I haven't tested them. I use standard plastic bottles with screw-on tops for repackaging milk and juices. They work fine as long as I keep them upright when packing and stowing. Otherwise, they are liable to leak if squished or tipped.

Glass is heavy to carry, hard to stow safely, and breakable. Snag a few of your handy canvas totes and distribute the six-packs and bottles evenly amongst them. Protect glass items by surrounding them with boxes, plastic bottles, paper goods, and puffy bags of chips. (Don't worry about crushing chip bags. If they can survive a supermarket, they can survive a dinghy ride to your boat.) Liquor bottles are the only exception to my "no glass on board" rule.

Store Refrigerated Food Properly

CONDIMENTS Buy the smallest sizes you can find of condiments such as mustard, mayonnaise, and catsup and, if you have the space, store unopened jars unrefrigerated on your boat until you need them. Most of these items need to be refrigerated once opened, so if you have an ice chest, use it to transport perishable spreads and seasonings home at the end of each trip. When I know I'll need only small amounts of things, I fill tiny plastic, airtight storage containers from my larger jars at home. If I can't distinguish one item from another, I label the container. Group the small containers in a supermarket plastic bag or nylon net bag for travel. Refill them as needed.

> HE SAID: *"This sandwich tastes like cardboard."*
> SHE SAID: *"We're out of mayo."*

DAIRY PRODUCTS Chunks of cheese, cream cheese, dips, and margarine tubs can be grouped in a plastic grocery sack or net bag with handles. Sticks of butter or margarine are easier to manage and serve if cut in half and placed in a small plastic container. Store sandwich meats and cheeses separately in small sealable bags. I like to place these items in a rectangular plastic container so I can move them around the ice chest on the boat without worrying about smashing them or getting them waterlogged.

MEAT AND POULTRY Items such as steak, ground beef, and chicken must be handled with care. Whenever possible, I pack them while they're still frozen. Wrap the food tightly in foil, and then place it in a plastic bag to prevent juices from oozing onto other supplies as the meat defrosts. Store meat in the coldest part of your cooler or ice chest. Unless I plan to cook the meat that day, I place it on a shelf under an ice bag or block of ice to ensure it stays as cold as possible, as long as possible.

FROZEN FOOD Make it a habit to freeze at home anything freezable that you plan to take to the boat. Cans of juice, jugs of water, bagels, bread, and meat can all be frozen ahead of time and used to chill your cooler for the ride to the marina. I also pre-chill all of the soda, beer, and white wines I take to the boat, and supplement them with ice packs and ice. Transport the whole bundle into your boat's ice chest and you'll have a head start on the chilling process. As a bonus, you'll have that cold beer ready once you've unloaded.

ICE At some point, you will have to transport ice to your boat. The farther you have to travel with ice, the longer you will have to worry about keeping it solid. In very warm weather, ice has a particularly short life span, so be prepared to stash it into a cooler for trips of any length. Otherwise, carry it short distances in canvas totes.

If your home refrigerator has an automatic icemaker, you may want to fill plastic bags with cubes and store them in your freezer. You can also make your own blocks by filling empty water jugs almost full of water and freezing them at home. Use the frozen jugs of water as you would ice blocks in your cooler. They last longer than cubes, and you can pour off the water for drinking as it melts.

Most often, it is easiest to buy ice at a marina or a nearby store. Blocks or bags are typically available in five-pound packages, ranging in cost from $1.50 to $3.00 or more per bag. The fancier the marina, the more expensive the ice. Some marinas deliver ice to boats, but be prepared to tip the dock attendant, as well as pay a modest delivery charge. Some days, such luxuries are worth it, no matter how much they cost.

Some boaters use dry ice as a supplementary refrigerant, placing it at the bottom of the ice chest or boat freezer to keep the temperature consistent and to maintain the solidity of ice blocks and cubes. Dry ice won't work for cocktails, though. If you plan to use it, remember that it is toxic and requires special handling—take the time to understand the necessary precautions.

Safer ice alternatives are the commonly used plastic-encased gel blocks that harden in a freezer. These are relatively inexpensive and will withstand repeated use. Look for new-on-the-market, flexible, quilted ice packs, which are larger and flatter and will stay cold longer than plastic-encased ice packs. They can also alternate as heat packs when nuked in a microwave oven.

SHUTTLING PERISHABLES

HE SAID: *"What's that smell?"*

SHE SAID: *"You forgot to empty the cooler last time."*

Packing refrigerator items and getting them to your boat unspoiled can be a problem. A good onboard refrigerator is a blessing you will greatly appreciate once you've paid your dues by struggling to keep food cold and safe to eat while using a cooler or an ice chest for a few years. The average boat, however, is equipped with an ice chest. Each weekend you'll transport the same perishable items back and forth because you can't leave them unchilled for a week or more. Make the process foolproof by creating a weekly "don't forget to bring to the boat" list. Soon you'll notice that the same list works week after week. Tack your list up in your kitchen and run through it as you're packing those last items.

Here's mine:

○ Mayonnaise

○ Mustard

○ Butter or margarine in a tub

○ Lettuce, prewashed and in a sealed bag from the supermarket

○ Tomatoes

○ Onions (optional)

○ Bread

○ Milk

○ Juice

○ Soda

○ Eggs (optional)

○ Lunch meat

○ Cheese

○ Limes, lemons

○ Ice

Take a tally each time you leave your boat so you can replenish wisely. Thirst is a by-product of being on the water. Water, soda, juice, and, of course, the booze aren't perishable, but they disappear as if they were. These items will likely remain a constant on your weekly list. Unless your boat is equipped with refrigeration and you have access to dockside power, you will need to bring enough ice to cool your perishables as well as your cocktails. After all, what's a drink without the tinkle of ice cubes?

CHAPTER

2

Figuring Out What You'll Need

LISTS, LISTS, AND MORE LISTS

If this is the first boat you have owned, and you want to outfit it, think simple! Start with the bare essentials, and then make lists and more lists each time you go aboard, enhancing and fine-tuning your inventory of provisions and gear. You will find that some items needed early in the season when the weather is cool are excessive baggage as the weather warms. Space is at a premium on any boat, so take unnecessary items home to make room for those you really need.

For example, in the spring and fall you'll need extra jackets, fuzzy warm fleece sweats, cozy wool blankets, and quilts. As the summer heats up, you'll work up a sweat just looking at these things. Take most of them home and enjoy using the extra locker space for snorkel gear, swimsuits, and beach towels. Making and using lists will help you manage your inventory. By the time torrid summer days dwindle into late fall snowflakes, you will have established a packing pattern, your boat will be perfectly equipped, and you will have figured out exactly what you need. Save these lists. They will come in handy next season.

If your boat has sleeping accommodations, chances are you won't be satisfied with simple daysailing. To prepare for overnight stays, make sure you have appropriate provisions, gear, clothing, and linens on board.

Our idea of a real boating vacation is not to have to use the car for the entire weekend, so we try to make sure we have everything we need before we get on the boat. After all, what's a sandwich without lettuce, tomatoes, and mayonnaise? Try doing without even the smallest essential for a weekend and you'll see what I mean. You may be able to get to a convenience store, but you will pay a premium and have a limited selection. Besides, who wants to bother shopping once you're settled and snug on your beloved boat?

Each time you leave your boat, headed for home, jot down a list of things you'll need to buy or bring for the next time. If you are the really organized type, create on your computer a master checklist of commonly used items and make several copies to keep on board. Fill one out each time you leave so your return list will be complete. List the clean clothes, linens, and nonperishable food you already have on the boat so you won't duplicate them. Create your shopping list from your inventory—be sure to include sizes and quantities—and replenish items that are low or depleted.

WHAT CLOTHES SHOULD I BRING?

Envision your weekend, then prepare for the worst! Count the days you will be gone and make sure you have enough changes of clothes (especially underwear) to accommodate everyone for any and all potential conditions. Because you will have to be prepared for all varieties of weather shifts and water infiltration, you will find these extras add up even if you are very selective.

Will you be entertaining? Are guests sleeping over? What are your plans? Do you need grungy clothes for cleaning and fixing up the boat? Are you cooking aboard, or will you be dining at a local restaurant? If you are planning to sail into a port, know the dress code. In New England, upscale ports, such as Newport, Edgartown on Martha's Vineyard, or Nantucket require nicer attire than marvelously casual Block Island.

Listen to the weather forecast. People who have to commute an hour or more to their marina often find different weather conditions than those they left at home. While still at home, check the weather reports for your sailing area in the papers and on television and radio to help you prepare for your trip.

Forecasts are updated several times a day and advise you about the sea conditions and weather fronts that you might encounter under way. Listen to the weather reports for your marina, for the area where you will be sailing, and for your destination. If you can access the marine weather channel from home, you can even better anticipate what to expect.

Preparing for the unexpected is a good battle plan when thinking about what clothes to take to your boat. Will it be warm enough for swimming? Is it supposed to rain? Do you have enough warm or weather-tough clothes for you and your crew? Extras for a guest that forgot them? Are you prepared to launder a few items should your stay be extended, or if you miscalculated your needs? Plan carefully and avoid the horrors of being without.

> HE SAID: *"There is no underwear in my duffel."*
> SHE SAID: *"Oops!"*

Managing Your Clothes Aboard

Chances are you will live out of your clothes duffel for the duration of a weekend trip. Boats, even the expensive ones we can't afford, often have tiny, odd-shaped drawers and cupboards. So if you do plan to unpack, be sure you have a designated place to stow your clothes or you'll spend all of your time tripping over the unstowed gear. It's nice if you can allot each person his or her own bag, because everyone's packing style is unique. A large or extra large bag will normally suffice for a weekend. If there are laundry facilities at your stopover ports and you don't mind giving up sightseeing time to babysit a load of laundry, you may be able to bring fewer clothes and pack lighter.

> SHE SAID: *"Shall I bring my blue silk dress and pumps?"*
> HE SAID: *"Nah, we're not going anywhere fancy!"*

Leave fussy stuff at home. You won't want to iron, even if you can. Remember—you're on vacation, so simplify. Stick to cotton knits or fabrics that pack well and can be rolled or folded easily into a duffel. You might want to coordinate an outfit or two for shore trips: jeans, shorts, T-shirts, leggings, and sweats are standard nautical lounge attire (and most likely what you'll sleep in). If you must hang clothes in your lockers, use plastic hangers. Metal hangers, unless they're stainless steel, will eventually rust and ruin your clothes.

Commission a space to store an extra set of underwear and socks as well as spare jackets for each member of your crew. If you have room, add a bathing suit, T-shirt, shorts, sweatshirt or sweater, jeans, sweatpants or leggings, and shoes for each person. A guest or one of your crew may need something dry and warm, or something light.

I always keep a small supply of detergent, bleach, and my favorite nonchlorine brightener on board to make trips to the Laundromat simpler. Buying these items on the road can be expensive and may create a storage problem. You may find yourself more than once burdened with bigger-than-life sizes of detergent you don't like and wouldn't stow anywhere on your boat, or get stuck having to buy costly one-load sizes of detergent from the vending machine at the Laundromat. I prefer liquid detergent because powders don't always dissolve in the cold water you're apt to be using, and it's also good for hand washing garments.

HOW ABOUT TOWELS AND BEDDING?

Yes, you'll need towels. But be forewarned: they can get used up pretty quickly on a boat and take a long time to dry, so I advise you to monitor their usage. Dole out one towel per person and insist that they hang it to dry, then reuse it. Kids are particularly bad about abusing towel privileges and will grab a fresh towel for every swim, leaving moist heaps of used ones about. I always hide a few extras aboard and guard them with my life for those times when every towel on the boat is soaking and we have yet to take our showers. Spoil yourself with extra large bath towels and you will always have a spare blanket for the cockpit on a windy sail, or something to lie on should you pull up to a sandy beach.

Although I love thick, luxurious towels, on the boat I use inexpensive, thin terry towels. They dry quickly and are easier to stow or stuff in a boat bag for the shower. If you're in the market for new

towels, take a look at the new swim towels that are super ab-
sorbent, yet dry quickly. These towels can be ready to reuse in less
time than usual and may save you some extra laundry in the
process. Bring a few hand towels to hang in the head, throw in a
couple of dishtowels for your galley, and don't forget potholders
and oven mitts for the barbecue. The captain will try to raid your
towel stash for his mopping and cleaning chores, so take along
some old towels or cleaning rags for these purposes.

Bag the Sleeping Bags

I can always spot new or occasional boaters because they sleep in
sleeping bags. If you're anything like me, though, you'll get tired of
being confined to a cocoon after the first few times. Sleeping bags,
although a great convenience, do not allow you to toss the covers
on and off and wiggle around as much as blankets and sheets do.
Kids equate sleeping bags with camping out and fun, so they are
more apt to enjoy their sleeping bags throughout the boating season. Certainly, sleeping bags are a staple to keep on board for that
extra guest you plan to berth in the cockpit. But for you? No, no, no.
If you are sleeping aboard a couple of nights or a week or more, you
deserve the same com-
forts you have at home.
Grab a set of king- or
queen-sized sheets and a
cozy blanket. Pack your
fluffiest pillows and enjoy.
Flannel sheets are wonderful
on a boat because they feel
dry when the air is sticky and
warm when it's cold.

To save space, let an un-
zipped sleeping bag laid flat do
double duty as an extra comforter. Compress sleeping bags
into tight little rolls and store
them in their sacks. Rolled sleeping bags make good bolster pillows
for the saloon or cockpit, yet they

are available when needed for extra warmth and for extra guests. If you use your berth to store bulky odd items such as anchors, extra sails and lines during the day, it may not make sense to leave it made up. In that case, store sheets and pillows in pillow shams and use them as throw pillows on board. If you are handy, you may even want to sew your own bag and pillow covers to match your boat's decor. There are so many hard areas on a boat that it's always nice to have something soft to rest against.

A more expensive, but convenient, alternative is a sleep system; that is, a berth-shaped bag with removable sheet and blanket inserts. Although I find these akin to sleeping bags, I admit they are a tidy solution for tight cabins because they can be rolled away when not in use. Costs range from $150 to $200 in marine stores or through catalogs.

Packing Linens

I pack towels and bedding in a separate duffel bag with a pull string opening at one end that doubles nicely as a laundry bag once it's unpacked. I hang my laundry duffel for dirty clothes on a hook and, at the end of the weekend, I zip it up and take it home. This method will also work with a standard duffel as long as it has handholds on the end so you can hang it up. At home, I keep my duffel bag in the laundry room and repack it with the clean towels and sheets I plan to take back to the boat. Throw pillow covers and pillow shams make good transport bags and leave one less thing to unpack or stow when you get on board. If you have space on your boat, tuck a change of bed linens in with those extra towels you've reserved. You can also keep extra blankets and pillows stored in zippered plastic blanket bags or trash bags stowed away in lockers.

Remember, if you are too warm, you can throw off covers and take off jackets and sweatshirts. However, if you are too cold, you're doomed unless you have enough blankets and clothes to cuddle up in.

DO YOU NEED TO BRING A COOKING SOURCE?

I discuss this subject more extensively in Part Three, *Food on the Fly*, but for your preliminary packing, you need to give this subject some thought. What are your boat's cooking facilities? Most boaters enjoy a barbecue grill. If your boat is not equipped with one, take a portable grill. You can purchase at a supermarket or hardware store inexpensive one-use grills that are already stocked with charcoal, or you can drag up that old hibachi or minipropane grill from your basement. Don't forget to pack the charcoal, lighter fluid (or propane canister), matches and, of course, the paper plates.

YOUR BOAT'S FIRST AID KIT

The first aid kit on your boat is the foundation of medical care for you and your crew. The longer you plan to be offshore, the more extensive the kit should be. Review your kit at the start of each boating season and replace expired, rusty, or incomplete supplies. You should find small packets containing most of what you will need for a variety of minor emergencies such as stings and slivers. Be sure you have compresses. I like to leave my first aid kit intact for emergency care. As you use items, it's important to replenish them so your kit will remain complete. A handy item to add to your kit is a first aid booklet. Keep everything together.

In addition to our onboard first aid kit, I make up a travel medicine bag in a waterproof, zippered cosmetic bag that I keep in the head so anyone who needs it can dive into it. I pack it with standard over-the-counter medicines and small sizes of items that I reach for most frequently at home or might take with me if I were traveling.

A typical medicine bag contains the following:

○ Ibuprofen or aspirin-based products to relieve headaches, fevers, and soreness (add children's strength if you have kids)
○ Lozenges or spray for sore throats

○ Antibiotic cream to prevent infection
○ Chewable pills for seasickness
○ 1 pair acupressure bands to prevent and alleviate seasickness
○ SPF 15 or greater waterproof sunblock and lip balm
○ Aloe to soothe sunburn
○ Antihistamine for sun poisoning, allergies, colds
○ Medication for diarrhea
○ Antacids for upset stomachs
○ Anti-itch cream for bites or allergic reactions
○ Soothing ointment for "wet bathing suit" irritation and rashes
○ 1 nonmetal box first aid strips (contents may be transferred into a resealable waterproof bag)
○ Alcohol or other antiseptic for cleaning minor cuts or cooling an itch

OTHER ESSENTIAL TRAVEL ITEMS

I keep a second set of our basic grooming aids and my favorite cosmetics on board so we have one less thing to tote back and forth each week. I also like to keep a spare 110-volt AC hair dryer on board. There usually is a source of power somewhere, even if you're not at a dock. Forget about purchasing a 24-volt DC hair dryer. The 24-volt battery input on a boat is comparable to the cigarette lighter in a car. There isn't enough wattage to dry your fingernails, and your hair will get tangled in the vents. Letting your hair air dry, though, isn't all that bad. Once you get used to it, you will enjoy not having to fuss with styling.

SHE SAID: *"The power just went off."*
HE SAID: *"You're not running the hairdryer, are you?"*

Your marine head wouldn't be complete without a supply of tampons and sanitary pads. I store them in a small waterproof, zippered cosmetic bag. Women guests appreciate the convenience in an emergency, and you'll be prepared for offshore protection.

CLEANING SUPPLIES

A few basic supplies will allow you to keep the interior of your
boat spiffy. I keep the following items under my galley sink, or
nearby, so I can get at them without disturbing the captain's supply
locker.

- ○ Small bottle of chlorine bleach for cleaning, disinfecting, and
  killing mold
- ○ Small bottle of disinfectant for killing strong odors
- ○ Small box of baking soda for deodorizing ice chest and
  safely scrubbing everything from toilets to pots
- ○ Spray bottle of glass cleaner
- ○ Spray bottle of Fantastik or similar cleaner
- ○ Spray furniture polish for varnished teak
- ○ Furniture oil (Scott's Liquid Gold, for example), or teak oil
  for unvarnished, interior teak
- ○ Dish detergent
- ○ Laundry detergent
- ○ A Teflon-based product for cleaning and protecting uphol-
  stered cushions
- ○ Fiberglass cleaner and wax
- ○ Sponges, clean terry cloth rags
- ○ Rubber gloves, cotton gloves (optional)

A Few Cleaning Tips

INSIDE . . . The best way to keep the interior of your boat clean is to
not let it get dirty. Start at the beginning of the season by wiping
down all surfaces. Clean fiberglass walls and surfaces with a good
spray cleaner. If you are ambitious, add a finish coat of fiberglass
wax to seal scratched areas so that they will repel stains and be easier to keep clean throughout the season. For all-purpose cleaning,
prepare a mix consisting of a few drops each of dish detergent and
non-chlorine bleach in a quart of cool water. Empty all lockers, cupboards, and drawers. Wipe them down with a damp rag dipped in
this soapy mixture to sweeten them and deter against the forma-

tion of mold and mildew. Dry excess moisture with a paper towel or a clean, dry cloth and let the area stand open until all moisture has evaporated. This is a good time to clear out excess gear and supplies you won't use.

If the interior teak on your boat is unvarnished, oiling it several times during the season will keep it looking new. Although teak oil is the obvious choice, my experience is that Scott's Liquid Gold soaks into the wood better, leaves a healthy finish, and lasts longer. You will know when your teak needs to be redone because it will have dry spots. If the teak is mold spotted or dirty, wash it before oiling it. Use the same soap/chlorine bleach mixture described above. Scrub stubborn spots with a soft brush or a piece of terry cloth. If you have varnished teak, any commercial spray furniture polish will spruce it up nicely and protect the finish. Touch it up with a fresh coat of varnish if it starts to look drab.

At the beginning of each season, I usually wipe down all the cushions on our boat with a well squeezed-out cloth or sponge dipped in tepid water, to which I've added a few drops of detergent and non-chlorine bleach. This removes dust and freshens them up. Make sure the cushions are completely dry before putting them back in place. If it is a sunny day, lay them outside on end to air and dry. Complete this process by spraying the cushions with a stain-resistant Teflon-based protectant acceptable to your cushion manufacturer.

See the sections on ice chests, ovens, and heads for ideas about how to keep these areas clean.

. . . AND OUT Entire books have been written about maintaining the exteriors of boats. On our boat, *Joy For All Seasons*, I'm responsible for keeping the topsides waxed. I find that a combination fiberglass cleaner/polish works well; I even use it on stainless steel posts and connectors. For even coverage, use a damp sponge to apply cleaning products and waxes. Allow the wax to dry to a film and then remove it quickly with a clean terry or knit rag so it doesn't bake on. Rub with a circular motion to remove the product film and buff up the areas. I wear an inexpensive pair of cloth gardening gloves to protect my hands and nails during this process. When the gloves get icky, I either throw them away or launder them in the same wash cycle as the dirty cleaning rags.

There are two ways to treat the exterior teak on your boat. (With any luck, you don't have too much of it!) If you prefer the look of natural, oiled teak, you will need to clean it periodically using a messy two-step process involving a drippy brown cleaner and teak oil. In between cleanings, scrub the salt and dirt out of the teak trim with a brush and use a hose to flush it with a freshwater rinse each time you wash your boat. The other method is to varnish the teak. We have found that varnish outlasts teak oil. At the beginning of each season, we sand off the old varnish and put on two or three coats of fresh varnish. Our teak retains its color and fresh appearance all season.

When cleaning window glass on your boat—portholes, windows, and hatches—make sure that what you are cleaning is actually glass. Lucite-based materials, such as Lexan, scratch easily and should first be flushed well with water or cleaning products to remove crusted dirt and salt before you apply cleaner. I find that a commercial window cleaner works fine. Hand-polish the window with a clean rag or paper towel. After you have expended the effort to clean the windows, apply a coating that will allow water and dirt to stream off without spotting. There are several products developed for this purpose, including those used for car windows. You can find them at any marine store, market, hardware store, or auto dealer.

Treat clear vinyl windshields on dodgers, bimini tops, and soft cockpits with this same careful attention because they, too, scratch easily. Rinse off the dirt and then apply a vinyl cleaner with a sponge, rubbing gently to remove dirt and stains. If you are using spray, apply it evenly and then rub the vinyl with a sponge, using a circular motion, until the area is cleaned. I have found that Lemon Pledge, recommended by boat dealers, also works well as a one-step cleaner and sealant for vinyl windshields. Allow the product to dry for a few minutes according to directions, then remove the film with a soft, clean cloth. Vinyl cleaner is also good for cleaning cushions, the nonskid surfaces on the topsides (please don't wax these), fenders, and even rubber dinghies. If the dirt is set-in, you may have to rub the cleaner in with a soft brush to allow it to penetrate uneven surfaces and uproot the scum.

THE DOWN HAUL

Well, you are finally packed and ready to leave home for the boat. Picture this. You and yours pile into your car and bumpity-bump down to the marina. Every bit of usable space is packed to the gills, including your seat, which is a bit higher than usual because you're balanced atop a sleeping bag or duffel that won't fit anywhere else. You say a silent prayer each time you need to change lanes or make a turn because piles of stuff are blocking your view. But, you're on the last lap and all you have to worry about is getting all that gear onto your boat. It is really pathetic, though, that the first emotion you feel when you pull into the marina parking lot is panic. Will I find a cart? You check the lot in a frenzy. You walk the docks looking for an abandoned one. You even stoop so low as to follow some folks with a loaded cart to their boat to procure that magic chariot you need to transport your ponderous goodies to the water.

Conveying heavy items, such as dinghies, engines, boat batteries, and toolboxes to your boat can be almost impossible without a vehicle of some sort. The larger the marina, the farther you can expect to travel with your cargo, and marina-provided carts are often few and abused. Consider investing in a cart of your own or splitting the cost of one with a neighbor; they range from $30 to $300 and are available from marine stores or catalogs and local hardware or garden shops. Chain lock your cart to the boat for safekeeping, or pack the folding style away in your car. Whichever model you select, make certain it is sturdy and roomy enough to meet your needs.

If the dinghy dock is near the parking lot, you may be able to eliminate the need for a cart and load your supplies directly into your dinghy. Row or motor your dinghy to your mooring, anchorage, or slip.

In addition to our dinghy, we also own a Boston Whaler (my husband likes an occasional burst of speed), which we keep on a trailer at our marina. Just before we launch it, we load it with the contents of our car. It's an easy ride to our mooring, where we tie up and unload. The advantage of a trailered powerboat over a dinghy is that you can unload directly from your car to the boat—no need to find one of those dastardly carts. If you own a trailered boat, or know someone launching one, take advantage of the situation to transport your gear. You can pay them back with cocktails in your cockpit later on.

Be alert to any and all opportunities to make packing and unloading gear easier, because it's a long haul.

> HE SAID: *"Did you bring the boat keys?"*
> SHE SAID: *"I thought you had them!"*

END OF THE SEASON

One of the saddest times of the boating season is when the air chills and the leaves turn a golden orange. It's time to put the boat to bed for the winter. When I didn't know any better, I carried home everything I had brought to the boat. What a chore. Each load weighed me down with more than poundage; it underlined the fact that this was *it*. I would have to resume being a normal person, dust off my make-up case, and go back to wearing pants with waistbands and shirts that tucked in.

After our first boating season, we took the entire contents of our boat home—life preservers, rubber hoses, extra lines, food, clothes. It was like moving out of a house. It took several carloads and too much labor. I was appalled at how much stuff we had collected in such a short time. Our basement at home looked like a Dumpster. Despite our intent to sort everything out, once the jumble of boxes and boat bags hit the house we were so glad the boat was empty that we left them sitting where they fell until the following spring.

Eventually I learned that it is not necessary to take *everything* home. Now, I leave the dishes, pans, and utensils on board. It's easier for me to run them home in a canvas bag at the start of the season for a good washing in the dishwasher than to trip over them all winter in my basement. I remove all liquids that may freeze (and explode all over the locker) such as soda cans, water bottles, condiments, canned goods, and cleaning supplies.

Alcoholic beverages do not freeze, so you can leave your rum on the boat for a warm welcome next season. Products such as suntan lotions, though, which lose potency when frozen, should be removed. Dry goods, such as tea, coffee, soup mixes, and spices, won't be harmed if left on the boat during the winter, especially if they are foil-wrapped or packaged in a zippered container. If you forgot something, it most likely will be apparent in the spring.

I suggest taking all linens—towels, blankets, sheets, pillows, and clothing—home to launder them. No matter how careful you have been, they usually reek of boat odor and will need to be cleaned or aired. If you won't need these items at home over the winter, you may wish to save this chore until spring.

Foul-weather gear and sailing gloves are usually pretty rank after a season of hard use and need a soap and water cleaning. I machine wash mine (even though the manufacturer may caution otherwise), using a gentle cycle, mild detergent, and some non-chlorine bleach. Sometimes it's the only way I can get them clean. If your marina has laundry facilities, you may want to skip hauling everything and clean these items on premise. It's not important where you launder these items, just that you do so at least once a year.

Hang freshly laundered foul-weather gear to air-dry, or run it through the dryer as you would delicate items, using a low heat cycle. I usually air-dry my sailing gloves over faucet knobs; they dry a bit stiff, but soften once I wear them. During the boating season, use a garden hose to rinse foul-weather gear that has been splashed with salt water and allow it to dry completely before closing it away in a locker. Unless you will be using your foul-weather gear during the winter, you can leave in on your boat after it has been cleaned.

Refresh your boat shoes by washing the salt off with warm water and a mild detergent. Use a soft brush for ground-in stains. Rinse the shoes with a hose and let them dry in the sun (or on the dock or at home), stuffed with newspaper to keep their shape; they

will dry like new. Seasoned boaters seem to collect boat shoes—
they never wear out. And if they do, just check out the backs of
boating magazines for a list of places where you can send your old
shoes to get refurbished. I enjoy my Docksiders year-round. An old
pair are great for yard work and for slopping around in the rain at
home.

If you are planning to charter a boat somewhere warm during
the winter, remember to remove your sailing gloves, beach shoes,
snorkel gear, foul-weather gear, and anything else you might wish
to take on your vacation. It isn't much fun trying to get these things
off your boat in the cold of winter when your boat is sitting 20 feet
off the ground on its winter cradle, buried under a snow-coated
canvas tarp. We've done it, we know. Ask yourself how important
those items are to you. We've never bothered to retrieve sailing
gloves we've forgotten, but we've struggled midwinter through ice
and worse to get the battery-operated blender off our boat so we
could make piña coladas on our charter vacation. I guess we all
have our priorities.

Cushions can stay on the boat, but tip and lift them off the
berths so air can circulate around them. Now, the captain will have
his own list of tasks that need to be done before the boat can be put
to bed for the winter. The water tanks need to be pumped dry and
flushed with antifreeze, as does the holding tank for the head. You
want to be especially careful not to be around on the day he services the engine. Changing the oil—a necessary end-of-the-season
chore—is very messy. You definitely don't want to be the one holding the drain-off container.

HE SAID: *"Here, hold this."*

SHE SAID: *"Ick!"*

My rescue from being the able-bodied assistant has come in
the guise of good male boater friends. Getting boats closed out for
the season and set up for the next has become a bonding ritual at
our marina. The men help each other perform the two-person
chores (leaving me wonderfully free to go shopping with the
wives). Unless you have Eskimo blood, going to the boat will become a hardship as the temperature drops. When you start to get
frostbite, pair your captain with a boat buddy to help him secure

the tarp over your boat while you wait in the car with the heater turned on high. Better yet, tell your boss you'll work weekends so you will be conveniently too busy to go to the boat—because by the time the captain has agreed it is time to put the boat to bed, it probably will be snowing.

3

Four-Legged Crewmembers

SHOULD YOU BRING YOUR PET?

You may have no choice but to bring your children to the boat, but should you bring your pet, too? You might be surprised to see pets of all types at marinas—cats, dogs, birds, and even pigs. The big attraction at Block Island (Rhode Island) one year was a little black Vietnamese pig riding up the dock in a boat cart. Apparently, the pigs are very smart and make excellent pets. Someone I know was just raving about having a ferret. Whatever happened to plain old cats and dogs?

If you have a pet you feel belongs with you on board, give it a try. Some animals adjust beautifully, and others freak out as soon as the engine roars. We used to bring our poodle to the boat and found her to be no problem. She was well trained, could easily wait until we got on shore for her walks and, as we sailed, loved to sit in the breeze with her ears being blown straight back. In contrast, friends of ours have a dog called Rudie, named after the famous lover Rudolph Valentino. I haven't figured that out yet because Rudie is female. Rudie is really skittish around the boat and has to be treated like a sensitive child. When her folks bring her boating, she's happiest prone on the dock, lying in the shade. Most boating weekends, Rudie is dropped off at doggie camp, where she picnics on hot dogs and hamburgers so mom and dad can enjoy sailing.

Copper, a large black-and-brown Bernese mountain dog, in contrast, is thoroughly at home on her boat. I say "her boat" because she runs the show. Her owner named his boat *Copperline*. What does that tell you? She loves swimming and rolling in the sand, which is not a problem until Copper is ready to board the boat and go belowdecks for a nap. *Eau de Wet Dog* can be overwhelming in confined areas.

We tried bringing our two cats, Smokey and Poogagloo,

aboard last year, but gave up on the project after two weekends of being awakened off and on all night and stepping in granules of stray cat litter that had made its way throughout our boat. I can't blame our cats for being skittish. They are indoor cats and, until this boat experience, the only place they had traveled was to the vet. Imagine what they must have expected after a one-hour car ride, followed by being wheeled, still in their pet carriers, at least one-quarter mile down the docks to our boat. The poor things were frightened.

Poogagloo didn't handle the boat motion at the dock very well and was too chubby to climb the companionway steps. We were worried about what he might do once the boat heeled. Smokey was better. Being more lithe, he jumped into the cockpit and performed a daredevil balancing act on our lifelines. But it was like babysitting two kids. We couldn't relax. I miss Smokey and Poogaloo terribly when we're away on our boat for any length of time, but I know they are safe and happy in their own little world inside our home. We hire a pet sitter to play with them and feed them while we're gone. And when we return, we've all had a vacation.

Birds are a charming and decorative addition to any cockpit. Many owners keep them hanging in painted cages or roam the marina with their pet parrots perched on their shoulders and chattering incessantly at passersby. I always thought having a bird uncaged a rather neat thing to manage, until I looked back after one fellow walked past me and spotted a familiar white dribble extending down from his shoulder. No thanks.

It's best to try pets out on the boat with short stays. Approach bringing them to the boat as you would any other excursion. Make

them feel at home. Pack their favorite toys and bring their food bowls and bed along. Place food and water in a cool area on a non-skid mat (self-feeders work well because there is less spillage) and give the critters their own spot to rest. One couple I talked with said their cat loves to sleep on a bath mat, which is a great idea because it can be easily laundered and has a nonskid underside. Another cat we know, Casey, has her own stateroom.

A cat will usually find a cubby on a boat that you never knew existed and will claim it as its own. A dog will commandeer the main walking area of the boat, your favorite seating area, or your berth. You need to be flexible. Although dogs can be trained to behave on a boat, everything I've read about cats aboard points out the risk factor of them jumping ship, getting lost, or following the smell of fresh tuna onto a fishing boat and going for a long sail. I love my cats too much to risk losing them.

POOPER SCOOPING

If your animal is aboard, you will have to deal with animal waste in some manner. For cats, try putting litter in a deep plastic storage box that can be sealed shut and stowed when your cat is off the boat. The new scoop-out style of litter is efficient because you do not need to replace it frequently. Filter out soiled clumps at least once a day as they become stonelike, or your kitty may rebel against using the box and make deposits elsewhere. Using a paper cup, collect clumps and other undesirable waste and enclose it in a plastic bag to discard in shore trash.

I have read that some animals can be trained to squat on the potty. This is an intriguing concept, but I question how it would work on a marine toilet. What if the animal lost its balance and fell into the blue disinfectant in the bowl? Cleaning him up afterward may be worse than picking clumps out of a litter box. I have always envisioned lowering the animal overboard to do its deed, but I have yet to test this theory.

Dogs need to be walked, of course, so you will need to consider your willingness to go ashore when their urgency arises. If you are on a dock, an early morning call may not be as inconvenient as it would be on a mooring—at least you can step off your boat without having to deal with navigating to shore in fog, driving rain, or turbulent waters. Many marinas have designated areas for dog walking (or pig walking, as may be the case). If this is not true of your facility, take your animal to a grassy out-of-the-way spot for his constitutional. No one enjoys having to sidestep brown piles in the parking lot or on the dock.

One default method of poop control that some boaters use is to maintain a grass-type mat on the bow of the boat with a line attached to it; when offshore, they train their dogs to do their business on this mat. The mat is easily cleaned by dunking it overboard,  holding the end of the line, of course. One caution on using this method—sunbathers won't be too anxious to lie on your bow, and dropping anchor may be a stinky job.

If you do have to ride your pet into shore via dinghy, at night or in fog or other inclement conditions, be sure you carry a flashlight and, if conditions warrant, a hand-bearing (handheld) compass to guide you safely back to your mooring. A friend of mine once had a frightening experience when she got disoriented one evening while attempting to row her dog, Shackles, back to their mooring. She inadvertently missed it and kept on going toward a light she thought was her boat. She and her small dog were located hours later on a small island offshore, cold and exhausted. Bringing along a compass and/or a portable marine radio might have helped my friend return to her boat safely. Finding your boat in the dark or in fog is discussed in greater detail in chapter 21.

KEEPING PETS ON BOARD AND SAFE

I haven't totally figured this one out yet. How do you keep your pet on the boat and out of the drink? There are several options you can try, depending on the personality and daring of your animal.

One couple keeps a knotted, thick hank of hemp over the side of their boat so their cat can climb back aboard should it inadvertently go swimming. I don't know if this would work if a cat were declawed. My vet recommends animal life jackets, which are a great idea if you can find one that fits snugly enough so your pet can't squirm out. (Good pet life vests are expensive.) Dogs will tolerate having a life jacket put on them more than cats will. You also might consider safety lines for them while under way. Dogs can go overboard just like people. Even with life jackets, neither dogs nor cats are a delight to retrieve. Dogs are natural swimmers, but I am not so sure about cats.

PART TWO

Conquering Inner Space

ONE OF THE FIRST THINGS that most of us discover when we buy our first boat is that we're too tall for it. As soon as we climb down the companionway we stoop to avoid hitting our heads—and we continue stooping over and contorting until we wish that we were made of rubber and our name was Gumby.

Training yourself to navigate around a boat is like learning a new dance. Once you get the steps down, you can do it faster and without counting the beats. You slip up less, too. We learn from our mistakes. A crack in the head reminds us to duck when getting up from our berth. We automatically give a wide berth to the starboard corner as we enter our cabin so we don't bruise our hips again. See? It's easy.

After a while, you learn to anticipate a few knocks and bumps from unforeseen obstacles and won't even remember getting injured until the purple-green bruises emerge. But don't worry, you aren't alone. Your friends will be sporting similar badges of "boaterhood," and your body will eventually learn where to duck and when to stoop. By the end of your first season, you'll be a pro.

At the same time you're learning how to maneuver around the boat, you'll find out that there appears to be no room to put anything, or do anything. This, too, sorts itself out as you get acclimated to your boat's inner space—its cabin (bedroom), berth (bed), galley (kitchen), saloon (living/dining room), and head (bathroom and shower).

CHAPTER

4

Where Is It?

WHERE TO BEGIN?

It's disarming, at first. Storage on a boat is rarely visible to the naked eye. But don't despair—space is there, just waiting to be discovered. Like moving into a new house, you'll need to get acquainted with all your boat's nooks and crannies before you can decide where you want to put things.

The best way to conquer a monumental task is to divide it into manageable chunks and then list the sequence in which to tackle them. Before bringing anything aboard, take time to investigate every inch of potential storage space—a job that's much easier to do when your boat is "naked." Remove every cushion in the saloon and on the berths and take a gander. You might be amazed at the wealth of lockers lining the hull. Don't, however, expect them to be convenient. Open all the lockers and drawers near the galley and note the amount of space available, as well as their sizes and shapes. If you know people with a boat just like yours, terrific. Ask them to show you around their boat so you can learn from their mistakes.

Easily accessible space on boats is precious. If some of the lower or side locker lids are screwed down, unfasten them to find out what's underneath. Some of them will contain boat workings, such as water tanks, waste tanks, batteries, and electronic gear. Use this exploratory time to become familiar with the location of these items. In an onboard emergency, there's no such thing as too much knowledge of a boat's inner workings. You might even hit pay dirt and find a locker you wrote off as used because it was screwed shut. Finding an empty locker is like finding a gold mine. A boating friend of mine found one such undiscovered treasure on her dad's sailboat after 20 years.

When planning your storage scheme, remember that most metals have magnetic properties that will deflect a magnetic compass needle away from North—so keep pots, pans, and tool-boxes away from your boat's compass.

SET PRIORITIES

When setting storage priorities, ask yourself a few questions. How often will you use the item? Does it need to be a fast grab? If you store it under the berths, will you need to undo the bedding to get at it? Think carefully about the sizes and shapes of the items you need to store and match them as best as possible to the available space, keeping in mind how frequently and urgently you might need them. You and the captain may disagree over who gets what for storage space—many captains will want it all—but pick your spots and stand your ground.

Obviously, you'll want to secure whatever storage you can in the galley and berth areas for kitchen goods and linens. Perhaps less obvious, though, is the space that's needed for navigational tools, such as pencils, plotting tools, flashlights, and handheld compasses. If you have a chart table, you're home free. If not, you'll probably do your chartwork on top of the saloon table or ice chest, so define a shelf, drawer, or other storage spot for navigational necessities. I stow our charts under the saloon cushions in a waterproof, zippered chart bag to protect them from tearing or getting wet; the waterproof bag also works well in the cockpit. The rest of your supplies? It's up to you. Just decide how deep you are willing to dig for them.

Once you've located all the available lockers, drawers, and cubbies and you've made some decisions about what will go where, I suggest placing sticky labels on each locker that lists what's inside so you won't have to take an entire locker apart only to discover that the item you are looking for is not there. If you are really organized, you may even construct a top-view diagram indicating locker locations and contents. Mount your storage plan in the galley, the underside of the chart table lid, or anywhere you can easily find it. Everyone aboard should know where to find this important list because it will enable them to instantly locate first aid and safety equipment. Of course, for this system to work, everyone has to return items to their assigned storage areas.

KEEP HEAVY ITEMS LOW

Keep heavy items, such as canned goods and anchors, as low as possible in the boat. If you're short on lockers, lift up the floorboards and check out the bilge (the holding area beneath the cabin sole). People who travel offshore for long periods of time or live aboard their boats are masters at taking advantage of every inch of space. They find the dry areas of the bilge a handy spot to store canned goods and other heavy items that will fit. The weight adds to the ballast of the boat and makes it more stable under way. Although the bilge might look like a trove of storage space, don't store anything there until you understand and observe the water drainage system in your boat. Never forget that the bilge is the lowest part of a boat's inner hull and therefore the place where unwanted water accumulates. If the shower sump overflows or a water tank springs a leak or an engine hose slips off its fitting, the bilge will become a pool. Any items that can rust, will; any paper labels that can disintegrate, will.

If you have to find space to stow an extra sail, check out the locker(s) beneath the V-berth. We used to set our spinnaker atop the V-berth until I found that it would squeeze into a large, inconveniently located locker underneath if I pushed on it hard and long enough.

Keep loose items from having too good a time dancing around cavernous lockers by grouping them into smaller containers. Sturdy plastic tote buckets with lids are good for small safety gear, tools, and cleaning supplies that need to be removed and carried. Unless the buckets are clear plastic and you can easily view the contents, list the contents on the lids to save yourself a lot of frustration. Plastic milk crates that fold to store are wonderful for containing extra soda, food, and supplies. Their flat, vented base keeps items off and away from irregular, possibly damp, surfaces. The slightly squishable sides of these folding crates allow you to coax them into oddly shaped lockers. (You'll find that all lockers are oddly shaped.)

SECURE FRAGILE ITEMS

Lanterns, binoculars, radios, and other bulky, fragile items you use daily need a secure spot to call home when you set sail. If you have no free locker space, snug them in the corner of a berth that's padded with pillows, blankets, or duffels, fashioning a way to lash them in place with shock cord or a spare sail tie. This may not hold up in heavy seas, but should work fine for coastal cruising. Most marine stores carry a large selection of teak and brass accessories that provide safe storage for these kinds of items.

I have a theory about keeping fragile items on a boat: they can't break if you don't have them. The only glass items I haven't been able to avoid keeping on board are liquor bottles. Even though some boats are equipped with liquor cabinets, they never seem to be large enough. Many have slots for all sizes of bottles— except the giant-sized ones that well-meaning guests bring. They— the bottles, not the guests—are a nightmare to stow. Find a secure locker or a dry spot in the bilge and roll glass bottles in foam, news- paper, cardboard, bubble pack, or some other padding material. Putting plastic soda bottles in between glass ones is another way to protect glass from breaking.

In the saloon you will often find space behind the upper seat cushions of the settee(s) that provide accessible, upright storage for tall items such as extra liquor or soda bottles, blenders, and toast- ers. On larger boats this space may be too wide or deep for snug wedging. If bottles and other stored items roll around, divide and conquer with plastic storage accessories.

WHAT TO DO WITH EXTRA BLANKETS AND LINENS

Dry, out-of-sight storage for extra blankets and pillows has always been a problem for me. Our usual two-person crew can easily expand to eight when the kids come to visit—none of whom ever seem to bring their own shower towels or bedding. For such occasions I stuff extra pillows, sheets, and blankets into large plastic zippered bags (the kind that blankets are sometimes sold in) to keep them both moisture and boat-smell free. I toss in a few fabric softener sheets for a fresh smell and cram the bags into a locker under one of the berths.

It's always a good idea to keep an extra blanket or two readily available to wrap around your legs when under way or to add to your berth on a cool night. Colorful pillow shams are a clever way to hide those extra blankets. Buy them, or make them, to match your saloon or your berth decor. Your boat will look spiffy and the blanket-stuffed shams make firm back supports for reading. They also look better than bed pillows when dragged into the cockpit for an afternoon nap.

HANDY HAMMOCKS

Small mesh hammocks are indispensable on a boat. They are practical for corralling lightweight, bulky items, such as paper goods, breads, clothing, and toys, and for keeping odd items up and off the berths and swinging safely while under way. A hammock in each berth area and one in the saloon should do it. Secure the hammock ends by tying them around overhead handholds. In berths where there are no handholds, screw sturdy brass hooks where needed, then loop the ends of the hammock around them.

Managing Clothes with Hammocks

For short stays aboard, assign each person a hammock in which to store laundry or hold once-worn clothing. Ask them to keep clean clothes stored in their duffel bag if there is not adequate space to unpack.

I always keep the clothes that have been exposed to salt air or worn once separate from our clean clothes so I don't have to launder the whole batch when I get home. Of course, if you have the luxury of drawers and closets, unpack. I like to line our drawers with fabric softener strips or cedar chips to keep clothes smelling fresh—but don't get carried away like I did one year. I lined everything, including our utensil drawers and dinnerware lockers, with softener strips. Our food tasted like scented laundry detergent.

Any shelves that are mounted outboard of berths usually have a small fiddle (lip), so you can pretty much count on your neatly stacked sweaters and jeans being spewed into unsightly heaps on the berths each time you go sailing. I got frustrated with picking up the mess every time we docked, so I devised a temporary fix for the problem by extending a net hammock across the shelf and in front of my stacks of clothes. I screwed two cup hooks several inches from the shelf's base, tucked the belly of the hammock under the lip of the shelf, and wedged it under a substantial heap of clothing. The contents of my stacks were visible, the clothes got air, and nothing spilled over every time the boat heeled. Although this method isn't perfect—the hammock's gathered ends leak a bit—it is an inexpensive way to alleviate the problem of the spewing shelf.

STOWING MISCELLANEOUS PERSONAL ITEMS

Someone is always coming up with new ways to keep things stored in confined areas. Scan catalogs and boating literature for ideas. Hanging plastic or canvas shoe bags aren't just for shoes. (Store your boat shoes in airy lockers or keep them together in a large basket.) Roll up T-shirts, underwear sets, towels, or sheet sets and store them in clear individual pockets or on canvas "shelves." A canvas shoe holder gives more ventilation than the plastic type. These bags normally have 10 or 12 slots, so they can hold quite a bit of gear when hung in narrow vertical spots. Make up small, portable kits for showering that can be hung or stashed neatly in the head.

Here are a few more tricks I've learned over the years:

○ If you shower aboard, install refillable soap dispensers

○ Those three-ounce paper cup dispensers that every supermarket sells can be mounted up and out of the way

○ Suction cup holders adhere firmly to smooth surfaces, such as fiberglass, and can be relocated whenever the spirit moves you

○ Marine stores stock teak accessories that hold toothbrushes, cups, and liquid soap

○ Use plastic organizers to divide and separate cupboards and drawers. (Make sure you measure the space so you can buy exactly the right pieces.)

Just like at home, small items seem to be always cluttering free counter space on a boat—the saloon or chart table are the most likely places for stuff to accumulate. Envision your boat tipping from side to side, or bouncing up and down, and think about where you might quickly secure items that you suspect will be going for a ride. One solution to flying clutter is to sew a couple of flat pockets with snaps or self-stick straps and secure them where small clutter collects. A variety of ready-made storage devices are offered in marine catalogs. Whisk loose items inside these mounted pockets to quickly stow them before getting under way. These pockets also double as permanent, movable containers for small items.

HE SAID: *"Where are those screws I left on the chart table?"*

SHE SAID: *"What screws?"*

KEEPING YOUR INNER SPACE SHIPSHAPE

The shipshape boat came about for good reason. Clutter in small, confined areas is as frustrating as it is dangerous. You move things from one pile to another and then trip over them. Your clutter sails with you, bouncing merrily off the interior walls of your boat. It's unsettling not to be able to find a place to sit or lie down. Don't give anyone on board any excuses for not keeping things shipshape. Assign places for everyone's gear and harp on them until they get used to putting it away. Their hammocks can serve as their private litter bins, as well as give you a spot to dump the stuff they may have left in the cockpit. Encourage your gang to put once-worn clothing in the laundry or in their designated berth.

First-Day Stowage Tricks

The first day of the boating season is the most frustrating one for stowing because you have to figure out all over again where things went last year. Of course, you experience a hint of this unsettling feeling each time you arrive at your boat for a stay. The piles are always there. The only differences are that the quantities of stuff have grown or shrunk with the length of your stay.

Even though you've thought through your needs and packed everything properly, mountains of boat bags and an assortment of oddly shaped gear the captain has added to your pile surround you. They are littering the cockpit, counters, and every other bit of existing surface space. You're getting claustrophobic because you can't make a move without stepping on or over something. What on earth are you going to do with all of this junk? You inwardly curse your boat's designer, who has got to be a guy, as you anguish about finding convenient spots to store the binoculars and the bread. No woman could ever design such poor storage arrangements.

HE SAID: *"Well, I have to run over to the marine store."*

SHE SAID: *"Before you go, where are you going to put all this gear?"*

Enlist everyone's help to get unpacked and stowed, but be quick about it—they'll all disappear once they have dumped you on the boat with the goods. If you've set up your ship right, however, you'll be stowed and ready to sail in no time at all.

Start by unpacking the galley bags. If you're getting ready to sail right away, unpack only the essentials and the perishables. Leave the rest intact, or put it into a tote bag—you can stow it later, at leisure. If you've got the luxury of a day or two aboard to organize and prepare for the weekend or season ahead, enjoy! If you will not be unpacking the coolers but plan to use them for the duration of your stay, leave them as they are. Your first priority is done.

If you will be unpacking the coolers, locate those dripping bags or blocks of ice you bought on the way to the boat, or brought from home, and clear a path to the galley. If the ice chest hasn't been cleaned, wipe it down before adding the ice—in the upper portion of the chest if possible. Close the lid and allow it to cool for about 30 minutes before adding any unchilled soda or warm food. If you have a refrigerator and it has been in operation while you were off the boat, drop in extra ice and unload the coolers. When you are through, pass the coolers up to the captain to get them out of your domain. You may wish to leave one cooler on the boat to use for icing beer and soda, or for keeping food cold for side trips. If so, find a flat, secure, out-of-the-way spot to store it so you won't smack your shins on it. (This is why those soft coolers I mentioned earlier are so handy.) If you have located a good place in the cockpit for the cooler, be sure to strap it securely to the base of your wheel or tiller mount to keep it from lunging and bouncing while under way.

If you will need to provide lunch or some other meal soon after getting under way (it seems it's always time for some sort of repast on a boat), you may want to dig out the bread and sandwich fixings before you unpack the remaining food bags. If you were clever, you made up the sandwiches at home or picked up some carryout food along the way.

If you are going to want to sleep soon after getting on board, you may wish to tackle your bedding and clothing bags after you have tended to the cold foods—the piles will still be there in the morning. If you are going for a sail right away, do your best to stow the bulk of your gear before you pull out of the dock. Pick the clothes and linen duffels up off the floor and flop them atop designated berths. Unpack the remainder of your supplies, stowing and stacking your empty tote bags as you go. Don't set sail with counters and cushions littered with tote bags brimming with supplies. If you don't have time to unpack everything, tuck the bags in snug nooks, under a table, or on a berth, where they are least likely to upset and go careening across the boat. Make sure you can access all the essentials you might need for your sail: charts, binoculars, sunglasses, and sun lotion. When you're all finished, make yourself a nice cold drink, stretch out in the cockpit, and enjoy the day.

5

Navigating Inner Space

THE ART OF BERTHING

When people buy a boat they are often more concerned about how *many* it will sleep than how *well* they will sleep. In addition to the standard berths aboard, you can usually house two extra bodies in the cockpit, particularly if the weather is fair or if the cockpit is protected. For emergency bedding, place cushions on the cabin sole—just remember not to walk on the sleepers if you get up during the night! There is always a way to accommodate extra guests. It's all in the stacking.

How many people do you want to squeeze aboard and how tolerant are they? You can't change the basic structure of your boat, but you can make the most of it by using comfortable bedding and learning how to cope with sleeping in confined areas, particularly if you must share a berth. Or, you can write a bigger check and buy a bigger boat, although larger boats don't always sleep more people—they just enable everyone to sleep in bigger berths, in private cabins, in more comfort.

MAKING YOUR BED . . .

Getting your bed made up is step one. If you're using a sleeping bag, just roll it out atop your berth and dive in. Before long, though, most boaters crave real sheets. They are cooler in the summer and much easier to wash, although lining a sleeping bag with a lightweight flannel blanket or sheet will help keep it sanitary longer. Once you've concluded that you deserve real sheets and blankets, you will be riding the civilization highway; that is, you will be beginning to think of your boat as your home—not as a campground.

Making up a berth with sheets and blankets can be intimidating and awkward, especially if it is an aft, quarter, or V-berth (which includes almost every kind of berth on a boat!), because many of these areas have low overheads. If that's true on your boat, I advise you to make up these berths *before* cocktail hour! You also won't want to tackle the job with a boatload of company or after dinner on a full belly. There you'll be, on your hands and knees with your rear end in the air, trying to tuck a sheet under the mattress you are kneeling on. It's a fighting match between you and your bedding, and no one wins. Take my advice and use a blanket to cover the disaster underneath (a fluffy comforter works best). Then forget about it. By the time you crawl into bed at the end of the day you'll be so tired you won't care.

If your berth cushions are vinyl, it is likely that you will wake up each morning with the bottom sheet wrapped around your knees, unless you cover the vinyl with a nonslip device, such as an egg crate foam, a blanket, or a mattress cover. Long sheet cinches that are used to keep bottom sheets securely in place are a great help. Look for them in marine stores or catalogs; they cost about $15. Crisscross them under your mattress cushion to secure four points of the sheet.

You'll find that there are no bed sheets in the world, short of that expensive custom stuff you can order at boat shows, that you can buy off-the-rack to fit the contours of your berths. So make do. Most double berths, particularly V-berths, require king- or queen-sized sheets. Use contour sheets as bottom sheets for V-berths and other double berths. Grab onto as many outer cushion angles as you can with the elasticized corners, starting with the farthest, hardest to reach, corners. Stretch the sheet across to the remaining areas and tuck under any excess.

To fit a flat sheet to a V-berth, knot together the two upper corners and slip the loop over the pointed part of the V-berth. Pull the sides down taunt and tuck them under, making sure there is enough sheeting left over at the wide end to tuck under the front of your berth. You will have to experiment with this some. For top sheets and blankets, gather up the bottom sections and tuck them under the narrow base at the bottom of the berth. Don't spread the sheet flat across or you will have no room to wiggle your toes under the covers.

For single berths, double over a flat sheet, sleeping bag style, and tuck it in on the side closest to the hull. Marine sleep sheets, comprising a sleeping bag made of sheets with a pillow insert, are reasonably priced and a good alternative for single berths. Remove any side or end cushions in the berth and you'll gain more sleeping space. If you have an extra guest, you can lay these cushions on the cabin sole for a makeshift berth.

... AND LYING IN IT

Figuring out how to get comfortable in your berth is step two. When we bought our boat, we never thought to ask the dealer how to sleep in our berths. We spent our first night on board with our heads jammed into the "V" of the V-berth, sharing both our pillows and our bad breath, a little too cozy to be romantic. We had no space to move our arms, but we had lots of legroom. It took us a few restless nights to reason that our feet belonged at the V end, which proved more comfortable except that you-know-who's legs are longer than mine so we had foot fights all night.

Getting in and out of most berths can be a formidable task, but a V-berth is the most challenging because it is raised about a foot higher than all other seating and berths. A small seat, placed at chair height, is often situated at the aft, or wide, end of many V-berths. With its removable seat cushion, it functions as a seat or a step up to the berth. To sleep, you simply remove the cushion and insert it so it is level with the berth. This leaves an open storage space below, which is good for shoes or clothes.

Climbing into a V-berth becomes unwieldy once the convertible cushion is in the night position because you've lost your "step." I recommend going stomach first. Using your arms, flop over the aft edge, getting as much of your body onto the berth as you can, then worm yourself the rest of the way until your knees are in bed with you. This is also how you have to mount the V-berth to make your bed. Be sure to bring all the bedding so you don't have to repeat this exercise any more often than necessary.

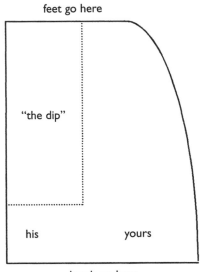

feet go here

"the dip"

his   yours

heads go here

As you might imagine, this contortion takes some planning if your mate is already asleep, enjoying all the free space. It's hard to avoid giving him a knee in the head as you try to jockey into position. To exit the V-berth, wheel your legs around to a semi-kneeling position, then wiggle down feet first. Getting out of the berth and back in again can be such a chore that you just pray, once you're settled, that your bladder will hold out until morning.

If your boat has an aft cockpit and you'll be bedding down in a berth beneath it, called an aft berth or a quarter berth, you will have a tad more foot room. However, you will need to be acutely aware of overhead space—or the lack of it—because the cockpit dips into these berth areas. If your boat is on a mooring or at anchor, you will sleep better in this type of berth than you will in a V-berth because boat motion is less noticeable at the stern. Aft berths are also less traumatic to crawl into and out of because they are at chair height.

The biggest problem I've encountered with aft or quarter berths is trying to avoid smacking my head on the edge of "the dip," my term for the interior portion of the cockpit that dips down into the berth. Depending on where the dip is situated, you could ram into it simply by lifting your head while scrambling around your berth. I've done this too many times. It not only hurts, but it is embarrassing to go back to work on a Monday with a darkening lump decorating my forehead. On previous boats with aft cockpits that we have owned, the dip dropped down just above my shoulders and hung so low I couldn't even roll over in bed, especially if I slept on two pillows—and I love pillows and use lots of them. Because I was smaller and shared the double berth with Captain *My Way*, I always got talked into sleeping under the dip. I know other women boaters who have convinced their mates to sleep under the dip by pleading claustrophobia. Maybe this will work for you.

Although an aft berth is a bit easier to get in and out of than a V-berth—you can just sit on the edge and swing your legs into place—the low overhead space can make bed making a nightmare because there is barely room to allow both you and the sheet to occupy the far corners at the same time. You'll likely become less fastidious about changing these sheets because bed making is such a hassle. If it gets too overwhelming, invest in a sleep system or revert to sleeping bags.

I whined so much about struggling to make up our aft berth that our next sailboat had a center cockpit, a design that is noted for its large aft cabin. Just think, a queen size-bed you can walk around, and no dip. Check out center cockpit boats and you'll beg for one, too.

I've failed to mention berths that are located at the sides of the saloon, or ones that can be created by dropping the dining table and inserting some cushions, because they are fairly easy to make. They are also straightforward to sleep in, particularly if you don't have to share them.

No matter where you sleep on your boat, get into the habit of remembering where you are before making any sudden moves. Clunking your forehead or rolling over onto the floor is not a good way to start your day. Each berth has its own best way to get in and out of. Experiment in the daylight and train yourself to use the same approach each time.

If you are sharing your berth, you will need to be assertive to commandeer a fair share of the space. Your captain, if he's like most men, will be a bed hog, sprawling his legs and arms as if he were sleeping alone. You'll be left slammed rigid against your side of the bulkhead unless you are proactive. Pretend you don't have any room and keep edging him over toward his side while he's still drowsy. Keep one knee bent at all times to maintain enough space across to allow you to roll over and change position. Stretch one foot toward the bottom of the berth to secure your rightful foot space. Your pillow and the extra width at the top of a V-berth will keep your head and arms free. Think space whenever you shift position and grab any extra that's there. And whatever you do, don't get up. Because when you return, you have to fight for your space all over again.

HE SAID: *"How is it that you grow when you get into this berth? You're half my size yet your head is up by my head and your feet are fighting with mine."*

SHE SAID: *"Magic, darling, magic. "*

WHAT'S A GOOD NIGHT'S SLEEP?

Is there such a thing as a good night's sleep on a boat? The challenge is ours. It seems there's always something trying to keep us awake, whether it's the wind whistling up a storm outside, the captain's elbow in our backs, or the party one boat over. Sometimes, of course, the soft, gentle motion of the boat acts as a cradle to rock us back to sleep. At others, we wish we were home sleeping in a bed that didn't move, in a house that didn't make noise. And when we're alongside a dock and the wind pipes up a bit, our boat thumps so loudly as it strains against the docklines that we've waken convinced we're attending a rock concert. We try to get comfortable but our bodies roll with every wave and thunk. If we are at anchor, the captain is constantly getting in and out of bed to make sure we're holding (while we snuggle deep and warm under the covers, pretending to be fast asleep).

Offshore sailors learn to cope with rolling sea conditions by wedging themselves tightly into a bunk when under way. On open-sided berths they use a lee cloth, a hammock-like berth extension, to keep from falling out and to enable snug, stable sleeping. Lee cloths are easy to install and can be tucked under the cushions when you don't need them. To duplicate this secure feeling in V-berths and aft or quarter berths when winds and turbulent seas are rocking, place firm pillows or rolled-up blankets alongside you to wedge yourself in. (Large body pillows would be perfect, except they would be a horror to stow.) A full duffel bag works equally as well.

Under stormy conditions, the berths nearest the center of your boat will be the most stable. If you are prone to seasickness, put on a pair of acupressure bands and take a motion sickness medication. With luck you'll get drowsy and drop off to sleep until the conditions improve. If noise is a problem, a pair of earplugs from a pharmacy should do the trick. The rubber type can be washed and reused. A boater friend of mine, whose husband snores atrociously, sleeps with a pair of soundproof headsets. A stormy night can be uncomfortable and sometimes intimidating, but unless your mooring pulls or your anchor gives way, you are perfectly safe.

Do You Have an Aching Back?

If you wake up in the morning feeling like you've been pounded with snowballs, chances are your mattress is shot. Most boat mattresses are merely foam cushions with no springs or fancy doodads to keep them as supple as your bed at home. The older boat cushions get, the softer and less comfortable they become. There are several ways to keep ahead of this problem and improve your comfort on a tired berth.

For a mattress that is too soft or one just plain old, consider topping it with a synthetic feather bed or futon. If you're handy with a needle, buy a mattress and trim and re-stitch it to fit your berth. Wherever possible, opt for synthetic fabric and fibers because they hold less moisture. Investing in these fluffy uppers is less troublesome than replacing the cushions in your berth (and they will give you the added support you need), because the next step is replacing *all* the cushions on your boat so everything will match.

If you want to soften a rock-firm mattress, start by purchasing a simple egg crate, foam mattress pad ($20 to $40). King or queen size will fit most double berths. Using a pair of scissors, cut the pad to fit the contours of the berth and lay it on top. As a bonus, you'll find that the foam helps keep the bottom sheet in place. Add to the ecstasy by topping the egg crate mattress with a pillow top mattress pad. You'll forget you ever had an uncomfortable mattress.

Deciding to replace a mattress tends to be the last option because, by that time, most of us will need new cushions for the entire boat—an expensive undertaking. Should you choose to order a new cushion for your berth, begin by researching options and comparing costs. Talk to your boat manufacturers to find out what they can do for you, and visit any local businesses that make cushions. (Some upholsterers specialize in making boat cushions and mattresses.) Boat shows are also a good source because a variety of dealers display their products at the shows. Orders taken at boat shows are typically discounted, so you may be able to get exactly what you want at bargain prices.

Your new mattress should be 4 to 6 inches thick and made of synthetic foam. Closed-cell foam floats and is stiff and thick enough to provide good back support. Old-fashioned foam rubber holds moisture, so forget it. Order in the fall or winter for late spring delivery and be sure to check on the progress of your order from time to time. My experience is that these folks need prompting, so hound the manufacturer for progress reports.

Don't overlook the fact that you can buy and replace the foam in your cushions yourself, a fairly simply project. A good fabric store will stock foam in 3-, 4-, 5-, and 6-inch thicknesses, and cut the pieces for you. According to a friend who recently made new cushions for her boat, the cost of a 4-inch thick, 6 x 4 piece of foam ranges between $80 and $100. If you can sew, make the cushion covers yourself or hire an upholsterer to complete them for you. Choose a sturdy fabric that has been coated to repel stains and mildew. Metal zippers will rust, so use plastic ones.

If you have major back problems, the best mattresses are custom-made coil mattresses, similar to the one you have at home. They can be ordered to fit the exact dimensions of your berth—the double mattresses are designed to fold over so you can lift them out of the way to get at those pesky under-bed lockers. Air mattresses with built-in posture support are also worthy of consideration. They can be ordered as a "short" queen to fit rectangular-shaped double berths. One manufacturer even hinted to me that the mattress dimensions could be customized. However, luxury does not come cheap. The coil mattress is the more costly of the two. I've never seen any boat show specials on either of these, but they are well worth the investment if you can't sleep on conventional boat cushions and spend many nights aboard.

ROMANCING AND OTHER EXERCISES IN FRUSTRATION

Boats are romantic—all that moonlight, silky water, and wine with dinner. That is, until you contort in your berth with 2 feet of head-room, banging everything except your intended. If you are alone with your honey on a mooring or at anchor, you might find the cockpit more forgiving—unless your neighbors have their binocu-lars out. Boater friends of ours thought that "doing it" in the cock-pit under the stars was private enough until they happened to be upstairs in the marina owner's office and noticed his telescope. It was pointed at their mooring area.

Ah, privacy. Eventually, we figure it out. We hang a curtain over the doorway to our berth and mount a matching curtain to the edges of its overhead hatch to avoid exposing ourselves to peering passersby. So they don't hear our moans, we learn to bite on a pil-low and have a good time. During the daytime hours, we discour-age company by posting a "napping" sign at our companionways and hope unwanted guests depart without noticing that our boat is bouncing. If the weather is cool or rainy, we close up the compan-ionway to fool people into thinking we've gone ashore.

Sometimes, the hardest part of being on a boat for an extended period of time is the lack of exercise. Pleasure boating is a perpet-ual vacation, a constant party. We eat more and move less (and wonder why rolls of fat exude from our swimsuits). We love it and long for it, but every once in a while we have to pull ourselves up short and face reality. Fitness counts. It energizes us to endure a hard sail, to winch in the jib under stiff winds, and to haul up the anchor if there's no one else around.

Although a short break from a regular exercise routine is usu-ally harmless, a summer of sloth will take its toll in pounds. Many of us don't exercise on board for several reasons (other than pure laziness): there's no room to maneuver, we are self-conscious about snickering neighbors, and there never seems to be a good time to do it. It's perfectly okay, of course, to take the summer off and clean up the mess in the fall, but if exercise is an integral part of your well-being and personal image, you can find the means to do it dis-creetly. Just plan your strategy.

Let your neighbors at the marina sit in their cockpits munch-ing on doughnuts while you walk or jog to the store for yours. No one needs to know you have an ulterior motive. Decide how much exercise you are willing to do on the boat. When might you do it? Can you power walk up and down all the docks? If your marina is in a picturesque area, the exercise can be quite enjoyable. Bring a portable radio and revel in the fact that you're not on a treadmill at home.

Keep your bike at the marina and pedal everywhere instead of driving. However, when you are sailing, it is easier to leave your bike at home. Bikes, even the folding styles, are bulky to stow and difficult to keep clear of lines and sails. In many popular ports, and especially on islands frequented by boaters, you can rent a bike for an hour, a half day, or all day. You can both tour the island and get your exercise in as well. If the water's warm and clean at your mooring or dock, jump in and go for a swim. If you're on a mooring or anchored, take the dinghy into shore and walk. If you are a strong swimmer you may even enjoy swimming ashore. Just remember that you have to get back. Every little bit helps. At night, after dinner, turn up the radio and dance in the cockpit or entice your neighbors at the marina to join you in line dancing. They'll be having such a good time they won't even realize they've joined your aerobics class.

Toning Up

Think "confined space." If you don't know how to do isometric exercises, get a book and learn. You can do them anywhere, and don't even have to move. Just smile instead of grimace and it will be your little secret. For upper body toning and strength training, keep a set of 2-, 5-, and 10-pound weights aboard. To save space, purchase the type that fill with water, or use canned goods. If you use cans, or other substitutes, as weights, make certain you can wrap your hands around them securely so they don't slip and dent the cabin sole. Look before you lift and be sure there's at least an arm's width of space surrounding you. Stick to weight lifting you can do while seated or lying down so there's less chance of striking something or losing your balance. And, if you exercise in the early morning or in the dark you might be able to avoid the titters of potbellied onlookers.

Calisthenics are a little more difficult to accomplish aboard because they require more space and are hard to do surreptitiously.

Check your berth area, the cabin sole, and the bow or cockpit for adequate space to exercise. Scout for a spot where you can stretch out full-length and extend your arms and legs up and to the sides without hitting something. If you opt for the bow, place a towel or mat on deck to absorb excess moisture. Fiberglass can get slippery, particularly with all that sweat you'll be working up.

My daughter's macho boyfriend, a nonboater who was staying on board with us, surprised us during our first cup of coffee one morning when he climbed up the swim ladder into the cockpit, stating he had just gone for a swim. We wondered at this because the air was cool and it was definitely not swimming weather. Later, we found out he had been exercising on the bow and had slipped through the lifelines. It shouldn't have been funny because he might've been injured, but he had been so arrogant about it we had to laugh. They broke up shortly after that trip.

CHAPTER

6

Invasions of Your Inner Space

TRASH THE TRASH

As if learning how to outfit and stow a boat, as well as learning how to live in a tight space, weren't enough, we discover that we have to share that precious space with things we don't want: trash, dirty clothes, and the unseen demon—bad smells. But like anything else in boating, we can learn to effectively deal with these nuisances so that we hardly know they are there.

I'd like to ignore the subject of garbage, but it keeps getting in my way. Trash is one item that none of us pack for our trips; we manufacture it as we go along. Most days, a nearly full trash bag will be sharing its bulk and its smelly little self with you and your crew below decks. It's usually lounging somewhere near the galley, although we all have our favorite little hideaways for it. If your boat is a rarity, one that is equipped with a proper trash receptacle, you've probably discovered a more productive use for that space by now. My trash bag is typically looped over a door handle or hung on a hook in a wet locker.

The most practical trash arrangements incorporate outdoor storage, for obvious reasons. Well-designed boats are equipped with a small trap door in the galley, which allows trash to be placed in a plastic bag-lined bucket in an outdoor locker. Thus, the trash and its odor are ousted from your inner space. Take a look at the layout of your boat; perhaps a carpenter can create such an outdoor arrangement for you. Many boaters store a small trash can under the galley sink or mount trash bag holders inside a cabinet door. My experience with the holders is that they don't have enough capacity and frequently spill or topple over. Hence, my drawstring-bag-on-the-doorknob solution.

Some fancy boats use compactors to keep trash under control, but compactors take up precious cabinet or other space. They also rely on boat batteries or electricity to operate (they're a serious power drain on small boats) and are notorious for breaking down and requiring frequent maintenance. According to the electrician who works on our boat, many folks become discouraged with trash compactors and remove them. As an alternative, you can manually compact your trash by crushing boxes and cans before disposing of them. Avoid messy leaks by selecting sturdy trash bags that won't be easily punctured by a pointed corner, or bottomed out when heavy. Like at home, you will want to discard your trash daily. Whatever you do, do not toss it overboard. Doing so is not only illegal, but environmentally unsafe.

If you plan to set out for parts unknown, trash buildup can become a real nuisance. While still at home, remove items from bubble packs and strip outer cartons. Transfer the contents of these packages into reusable containers or resealable plastic bags whenever it makes sense to do so.

Coast Guard regulations require all boats to prominently display on board a plaque that cites dumping rules. Read it and bawl. The longer you are offshore, the more trash you will accumulate. When the mound gets really large and offensive, it's time to take action. Stuff the trash somewhere outdoors where it can remain intact until you can properly dispose of it. One common solution is to place tied-shut trash bags in an outdoor locker or toss them into a dinghy to temporarily remove them from your living space until you can get them to shore.

Recycling

Recycling complicates the problem of trash storage and disposal. To simplify the process, I keep two bags or receptacles going on my boat, one for garbage and one for bottles and cans. Most mainland marinas will accept trash in these two forms. On small islands, however, dumping regulations are often stringent; their disposal problems are passed on to visiting mariners. On Cuttyhunk, Massachusetts and Block Island, Rhode Island, two popular stopovers for New England boaters, there are as many as six different shore receptacles for refuse. Boaters are required to separate green glass, brown glass, clear glass, cans, and paper from food garbage. A person can stand there all day figuring it all out.

To dispose of trash where recycling is encouraged, I just grab my food garbage bag and my bottle and can bag and take them to the dump. It's easy to find—I just look for the flies. It is definitely not a place to spend time deliberating. If I am faced with the "variety pack," I empty my can and bottle bag, piece by piece, into the receptacles provided. Reducing recyclables to a single bag saves storage space and eliminate having to dig through coffee grounds and rotted bits of the previous evening's meal to locate cans and bottles. Some marinas impose a fee to dispose of trash, especially if you are not taking a slip. When all else fails, just sling the bags in the dinghy and let them marinate until you hit a more appropriate disposal area.

It's always tempting to toss leftovers overboard. Who can resist throwing bread crumbs to the ducks or swans paddling around your boat begging for handouts? But, alas, even food garbage is prohibited by U.S. regulations unless you are many miles from shore. And even so, your trash may be the object of affection by a fish that's bigger than your boat. Finally, it's embarrassing to throw overboard something as simple as orange peels in an anchorage area and watch them float off to visit the neighbors. Food bits can be visually as well as chemically polluting, unless they are quickly biodegradable.

Sea life can get trapped or injured by the plastic rings that encase six-packs, and by the sharp metal loops on cans. Plastics and other nonbiodegradable materials just remain there, littering our ocean. Outside the U.S., follow Coast Guard regulations for

disposing trash in international waters. Most small islands in remote areas, such as the Grenadines, often burn trash and have no
facilities for recycling. You may be horrified to find they even
dump it into the ocean, but that doesn't mean you should, too. Be
considerate of our environment. Keep the water that's giving you
so much pleasure a safe clean place for our finned friends by disposing your waste properly. You can manage your trash. Just
show it who's the boss.

THE BIG PILEUP—LAUNDRY!

Boating blows through clothes like you wouldn't believe. In the
heat of summer you may go through several T-shirts a day or find
that your favorite navy blue shorts are crusted white with salt from
your last dinghy ride into shore.
   A few basics:

- Don't mix clothes that have been exposed to salt with ones
      that haven't
- Designate a place to keep dirty laundry
- Keep laundry supplies on hand
- Hang wet laundry to dry, carefully

   So, what to do with all those used clothes looking for a home
on our boat? Like the trash, the heaps of discarded, dirty clothes
can grow ugly as a trip progresses. Once items have been exposed
to salt water, they never seem to dry, even under the best weather
conditions; the salt in the moist air will leave clothes feeling
slightly stiff and damp. Clothes and linens that have been exposed
to salt air are contagious to fresh ones and will turn them sour. Resist the temptation to fold a sweatshirt you wore sailing all day and
place it on top of fresh clothes, even if it seems clean enough to
wear again. Instead, put it in a separate "recycle" pile.
   Locate an out-of-the way storage area to stow truly dirty
clothes that you don't want to see again until you've got access to a
washing machine. A ventilated locker or a simple clothes hook in
the head or a cabin will do nicely. Place dirty clothes in a desig-

nated laundry bag. A hanging, mesh bag works well because it is ventilated, thereby preventing accumulated moisture on clothing from forming mildew. I often use a spare duffel or canvas tote because I always have one available and they are convenient to carry home—just make sure you leave them unzipped so air can circulate. Make every effort to dry items before adding them to your laundry sack because dampness is a welcome sign for mold. And once clothes get speckled with mildew, they'll never look the same again.

Coping with Wet Laundry

In general, it's not good boating etiquette to hang an entire load of wash on the lifelines of your boat at or near a marina. It's not pretty and spoils the ambiance of the area for your fellow boaters. However, swimwear and shower towels are usually an exception. Swimming and showering are, after all, nautical activities. I keep clothespins aboard for this purpose and store them in a mesh bag that hangs in an out-of-the-way spot when I'm not using it.

I find that towels dry fastest when hung in a single layer, clipped with three or four clothespins. If it is very windy, I knot the tip of each item around the lifeline as an extra safeguard. Clothespins are notorious for blowing off and taking towels for a sail. And, because swimsuits are so expensive, and it's impossible to replace favorites, I don't trust mere clothespins to keep them anchored to lifelines. Instead, I loop our swimsuits around the lifeline, threading the straps or upper portion through the crotch. I learned to do this once when we had no clothespins and now I use this method routinely. Our suits have survived 35-knot gales, when the towels were left hanging by one lone clothespin. It's not smart to sail with clothing hanging from lifelines. It looks scruffy, the items are certain to get wetter than they already are, and you can almost count on the laundry blocking your vision on certain tacks or getting entangled in lines.

There are times when you must deal with a basketful of wet clothes. Perhaps everyone got caught in the rain or you don't have time to dry the clothes at the Laundromat. Whatever the reason, wet laundry poses a problem. Here are your options.

Wait to see if the next port has laundry facilities and dry your clothes there.

If the weather is sunny and dry, apologize to your neighbors and hang the wet items outdoors. Once the sun goes down in the Northeast, dampness sets in and it is useless to leave clothing outdoors. It will only be wetter in the morning, so take the clothing inside and re-hang it the following day.

Hang the clothes about the interior of your boat until they dry.

Most often, the third choice is what we must deal with. If you need to dry clothing indoors, choose a time when you are not expecting company because space will be difficult to navigate for a few hours. If it is raining, your clothes will take a long time to dry, even indoors.

Place the wet clothing on plastic hangers to make items more portable, and open hatches and portholes so fresh air can circulate. If you have small fans, turn them on. Hang the clothes wherever there is space for open-air drying, such as over the turn handles of hatches and portholes, in the companionway, or over handholds. Our boat has a row of handholds along each side of the overhead. One final hint: my unorthodox place for quickly drying lightweight panties and bras is to loop them over an open porthole. Just make sure they're secure. It's embarrassing having a helpful neighbor return your underwear, hanging dripping wet off the end of a boathook.

Laundromats

If you're on a coastal cruise, a waterway guide will indicate which marinas are equipped with laundry facilities. Although laundry facilities at marinas are often sparse and always expensive, they can bail you out when the only remaining options are to wear smelly clothes or go nude. I've paid anywhere from $1 to $5 to wash a single load of clothes. Dryers at one large marina on Block Island ask for a quarter every 10 minutes—and good luck finding a unit that works. Some enterprising soul could make a ton of money doing a wash, fold, pickup, and delivery service there. But then we would miss out on all that exercise hauling the clothes up and down the hill. I have found a few decent facilities at marinas along the New England coastline, though, and treasure them. A marina often has only one washer and one dryer, so you may find them available only during off-hours like early morning, midafternoon on a beautiful sailing day, or late in the evening. If you are desperate, you can always revert to the laundry facility that offshore cruisers rely upon—a bucket of soapy water.

CHAPTER

7

Inner Comfort

CLIMATE CONTROL

I can't help but wonder why boaters are so much more tolerant of weather conditions on their boats than they are in their homes. Maybe it's because we get in the camping mode and a little hardship seems a challenge. We can, though, take measures to ensure that our inner space is as cozy as conditions allow. One of the advantages to being in a small area is that we can easily effect temperature changes. With little effort and a few inexpensive heating or cooling devices, the inside of a boat can be a snug refuge from nasty conditions outdoors.

THE CABIN'S HOTTER THAN A HEARTH

The sun's been pounding your boat all day. It's four o'clock in the afternoon. You crawl onto your berth to hide from the heat and it's so hot you could roast a turkey on it. Start by assessing your environment. If you can't get your cabin cooled off by bedtime, you may have to sleep in the cockpit which is, incidentally, quite pleasant. Where is your boat located? Are you socked into a windless cove or slip? You will always be warmer at a dock than at anchor. The great part about a boat is its mobility. If you don't like where you are, you can move to somewhere else. Motor to a spot where the breeze is blowing and settle in for a cool evening away from the heat. Lower your body temperature by taking a swim or immersing up to your neck in the cool water surrounding your boat. Sponge off frequently with fresh water.

Include in your pre-season planning some money to buy cooling devices, such as windscoops, suncovers, and fans. At anchor or at a dock, a windscoop will grab any air that's out there and channel it into your boat. Windscoops mount, like a tiny sail, between the headstay and the inside of an overhead hatch. A hatch that's pointed toward the breeze will bring in the most air. Windscoops are inexpensive and easy to stow—simply roll them up and tuck them away.

A large, portable sun umbrella can provide some shade on a windless, sunny day; it can also protect you from a passing shower while you are docked unless, of course, it's real windy.

A suncover large enough to shade the middle to aft portion of your topside is important for keeping your inner space cool. A length of light canvas, a tattered sail, or an opaque plastic tarp can be used as a makeshift sunshade. Otherwise, construct one using two wooden dowels and a length of light-colored fabric, or order a custom cover from a canvas dealer. The suncover should be white or pale colored to best reflect heat, and large enough to at least cover the cockpit. You may want to extend it forward or aft of the cockpit, depending on your boat's design. Clip or tie it in place and don't forget to remove it when the wind picks up. (It goes without saying that you shouldn't sail with a suncover in place!) One stormy morning when we were anchored at Great Salt Pond in Block Island, my husband and several other nearby boaters were forced out in dinghies in driving rain to rescue a friend's boat that was sailing back and forth on its anchor. Our friend had left his suncover in place overnight; when the wind picked up, it filled the canvas cover as if it were a sail. His boat was on a collision course with neighboring boats.

Nothing, except air conditioning, beats a fan for circulating air on board. When alongside, plug in a portable fan to keep the air moving. While chartering in the Caribbean, we discovered the value of having a few small oscillating fans placed throughout a boat. When placed in each cabin and in the galley or saloon, these tiny fans, which run off of a boat's house battery, keep the air circulating and provide a breezy interior, even on the most vile of summer days.

Solar- and battery-powered ventilators, especially when used in conjunction with fans, allow fresh air to enter a boat. This is essential when all portholes, hatches, and the companionway must be sealed shut against driving rain. Look into adding vents in closed areas of your boat, such as the head, galley, and berths. You can never have enough ventilation on board a boat.

Air conditioning, the ultimate dehumidifier and cooler for your inner space, is a luxury. It requires dockside power and a generator or inverter to operate. Air conditioned boats are most practical in the south where high humidity and hot weather are sustained for long periods of time. In New England, we can usually get through the dog days of summer using a sun cover, windscoop, and a few fans. Finally, remember that an anchorage will always be cooler than a dock.

IT SEEMS COLDER INSIDE OUR BOAT
THAN IT IS OUTSIDE

You're right. It is cooler. A boat traps dampness. Everything feels clammy and you can't seem to get warm. Fortunately, a smidgen of heat on a boat makes a big difference. Boat interiors are usually so small that simply lighting a candle or an oil lamp, or heating up some soup or coffee, can pull the moisture out of the air and take the bite out of the chill. Cold, rainy days are a good time to turn on the oven and bake a batch of brownies. The combined smell of chocolate and the feel of the warm dry air will cuddle you like a comforter against the miserable weather outdoors. Cook some pasta, open a bottle of wine, light the candles or your oil lamp, and you're in heaven.

> HE SAID: *"It's miserably cold and rainy out tonight. Do you still want to go ashore for dinner?"*
>
> SHE SAID: *"Open that bottle of wine. I think I have a can of stew around somewhere."*

We get some gorgeous days in New England in May and October when the sun is so warm it lulls us into wanting to sleep aboard, despite near freezing evening temperatures. Swathed in heavy sweats and shrouded in quilts, we snuggle in for the night, suppressing any urges to get up and use the head. I refuse to get out of our berth before the morning sun warms our boat, and have perfected the art of faking sleep until I hear the captain arise and get the coffee perking. When my feet hit the cold floor I cringe, then crawl out of our berth, dragging my blanket with me. I head for the cockpit, clutching a warm mug in my cold hands, and am pleasantly surprised. It's warm! This is nature's gift. One of those magic moments that makes any hardship well worth the endurance. What a splendid morning!

There are several ways to keep your boat warm when you are anchored or moored. One is to use a wood- or coal-burning stove or heater. Their use will likely require your attendance at intervals—including the middle-of-the-night—to replenish the fuel.

An alternative is the use of diesel or kerosene heaters, in which the fuel is supplied automatically. Both types of heaters are available in attractive designs using brass, tile, or stone, which warm the appearance of your cabin as well as the air.

You can also use clean and odorless electric space heaters, but they require a very large supply of electrical power—in amounts that overtax most boats' batteries.

Generators are typically found on larger sailboats and powerboats. They can be noisy and the electrical benefits subside after you turn the generator off.

If you don't have any of this equipment, make it easy on yourselves and spend cool and damp nights dockside with a space heater hooked into shore power. This will extend your season comfortably and allow you to actually enjoy sleeping aboard in cold weather. Early and late in the season the docks are not full. If you are on a mooring, ask your marina for permission to keep your boat at the dock for a few weeks. If space is available, most will be happy to accommodate you.

CHAPTER

8

Are You Guilty of Boat Breath?

THERE'S SOMETHING IN THE AIR

The sour smell that assaults us whenever we open our boats after they have been closed up for awhile is one that is familiar to all boaters. I call it "boat breath." Discussing boat breath with friends is like discussing bad body odor, it's too embarrassing to share. The captain and I tried for years to cover up our boat's aroma. Each time we expected company, we rushed ahead to arrive a few moments before they did so we could air out the boat and give it a good spray of room deodorizer. It was always a race to get everything done, with people hot on our heels, without getting caught wielding the spray can.

Bad smells are a turnoff for everyone. If you've ever been home or apartment hunting and walked into a place that reeked of garlic or trash, I bet you didn't go back for a second look. Once odor attacks fabrics and carpets, it is difficult to exhume without thorough cleaning. Inviting people to our boats is like welcoming them into our home. We want them to stay, and to come back again. We want them to remember the wonderful day they spent sailing, not how awful our boat smelled.

Boat breath is stubborn. Although a boat can appear clean and neat, foul smells are often skulking in closed lockers and drawers, permeating our clothing, blankets, pillows, and sleeping bags. The longer these items remain on board, the stronger they smell. I know boaters who keep their weekend clothes stored in their car to avoid their being infected by boat breath. Others use a strong dose of perfume to cover it up. And leaving the boat doesn't always mean leaving boat breath behind. More than once, I've gotten a snootful of boat breath while unpacking duffels at home. So what can we do about it?

I tried in vain for years to eliminate boat breath, but everything I did merely covered up the odor rather than eliminate it. I lined drawers with fabric softener strips, hung deodorizers everywhere, sprinkled lockers with cedar chips, and sprayed room deodorizer on cushions and into open areas. My efforts seemed to help until we closed the boat up for a few days. When we returned, there was the old devil back to spook us, as if it resented our departure and had been saving up for payback. The longer we were away, the more violent the onslaught. I had resigned to living with the smell, assuming it must have something to do with the fiberglass, when we realized that our boat was only trying to tell us it couldn't breathe.

GIVE ME AIR!

When a boat is closed, moisture builds and creates a perfect environment for mold spores, which thrive in damp places. Warm weather escalates their growth because higher temperatures hold more moisture—which is why boat odor is more obvious in the summer. Mold and mildew are the culprits.

To attack this problem, start by taking a look at the ventilation system on your boat. Are there enough vent ducts to bring fresh air inside? Various styles of vents are available; one that we like has a built-in, solar-powered fan to coax fresh air aboard and keep it continuously circulating. A good vent will let air in and keep water out. This is important when the weather is stormy because you will be able to enjoy fresh air, even though you must shut all the hatches and portholes.

We found that, by leaving drawers and lockers slightly ajar and the ice chest cover open when we closed the boat, the odor attack on our return was substantially reduced. In addition, clothing and other odor absorbing items remained fresh smelling. When the boat is occupied, however, open doors and drawers are hazardous.

For a permanent solution, look for ways to allow air into closed spaces. Replacing solid cabinet doors with vented ones is a good idea, and is particularly helpful for wet lockers, which are designed to store foul-weather gear, lines, and life vests—making wet lockers real moisture pockets. Most wet lockers have drainage holes in the sole beneath them to allow water runoff from wet gear, but they remain a prime area for mold growth. If you leave wet items shut inside a wet locker for long, you'll be greeted upon your return by moldy gear and that horrendous smell.

The fronts of lockers and drawers usually have decorative ventilation holes cut in them; if yours don't, you might want to have some cut. Whenever you leave the boat for any length of time, it's a good idea to prop any cushions (on the settees and berths, for example) up and leave ajar any lockers that are underneath.

THE MOLD MONSTER

Here's the problem. This is a boat, and a boat sits in water. The air that circulates through and simply surrounds a boat sitting in water is likely to have a higher than normal moisture content. So, when that moisture hits a surface that's colder than it is (bulkheads and overheads are the most natural targets), it will condense—and leave droplets of water to wreak damage. (This is more of a problem with fiberglass boats than with wooden boats, but then wooden boats have other problems to contend with.) Even without condensation, air with high moisture content is conducive to the formation of mildew—and there isn't much we can do about it except ventilate. A boat is very forgiving, though, and most modern boats are made of materials that are as resistant as technologically possible to the effects of unwanted moisture. The dampness *will*, however, collect and threaten our clothing and supplies. Our job is to keep it under control when it invades our inner space.

When you first notice little black or green dust droplets lining the cracks and crevices of your boat—and you will—you'll know that the mold monster, the harbinger of boat breath, has arrived. It will look like dirt, but it's not. If you clean it using conventional soap and water it will seem to disappear, but it won't. You've removed the mildew and mold, but the spores live on. New little speckles will breed like guppies and you'll be swearing obscenities because boat breath will be back.

Kill It—Dead

To permanently oust mold spores, you must spray or wipe down the interior of your boat, using either a commercial mildew killer or one that you make yourself. Depending on air temperature and humidity, you may only need to do this once or twice a season, concentrating on hard surfaces, such as fiberglass and teak-lined areas. The most effective mold-killing products are chlorine based, so keep them away from nonbleachable items, such as upholstered cushions and dark-colored canvas and clothing.

Wear old clothes and rubber gloves for this project. To make your own weak chlorine solution, mix one capful of chlorine bleach with one quart of water in a small bucket or jug. Pour some into a spray bottle to use for touch-ups later. Using an old rag or sponge, wipe down all surfaces, making certain to soak the corners. Do one small section at a time. Swab the bulkheads, ceiling, and sole. Empty lockers and drawers and wipe down their interiors. Allow the areas to dry completely before replacing items and closing them. The best time to do this chore is on a dry sunny day. Never do it in a closed boat. You want to open hatches and portholes to allow the boat to air out and to keep you from getting asphyxiated from the chlorine fumes.

I have read that color-safe bleach will control mold, but I've found that it won't remove stubborn mildew spots, so I question whether it is deadly to mold spores. However, since a chlorine-based product will fade dark-colored fabrics, there aren't too many other options. I use a mild solution of color-safe bleach to clean my upholstered navy blue cushions; I wipe them down once or twice a season with a damp rag dipped in the solution and wrung dry.

To clean light-colored or white fabrics that have become mildew spotted, test a corner with a weak chlorine solution or a commercial mold killer before upgrading to stronger treatment. A fellow boater used a commercial mold spray on his white canvas bimini and found that it worked, while the color-safe bleach method failed. He had an initial scare when the white canvas turned yellow when it was wet with the product, but the canvas dried clear and clean.

Marine stores and hardware stores carry a variety of inexpensive liquid or solid water-absorbing aids that you can place throughout your boat once you've swabbed the interior surfaces with mold killer. If you have an electrical power source, plug in a small dehumidifier or a portable air conditioner. If at any time you notice water in a locker, don't chance storing anything you care about in it without first encasing it in a waterproof bag. If you intend to store clothing or linens aboard for the season, include a few drops of chlorine or color-safe bleach in the laundry to safeguard them from boat breath. Moldy odor is the most offensive enemy on a boat—fend it off before it takes over.

CHAPTER

9

Keeping Your Head

BE NICE TO YOUR HEAD

Let us not forget that odious but revered necessity aboard a boat, the marine toilet, commonly known as the head. A marine head contains a sink, possibly a shower, a mirror, and of course, a toilet; therefore, a person "going to the head" could be involved in an array of activities.

Depending on the size and sophistication of your vessel, your marine toilet may be a plastic bucket, a portable potty, or a luxury model with a built-in holding tank for its waste. True to form, the bigger the boat, the more luxurious the head. Regardless of its size or amenities, however, keeping a clean head of any kind is a challenge all its own.

There is nothing more embarrassing than emerging red-faced from the head and admitting that you clogged it. A head does not—repeat, does not—digest tampons, sanitary pads, cotton balls, cotton swabs, or gobs of toilet paper. Seasoned mariners believe that toilet paper, even in small amounts, creates problems. Whether your head is finicky or not, be cautious about what you put into it. Hang a small plastic trash bag in an inconspicuous spot nearby the toilet for easy disposal of nondigestible items. Use biodegradable white toilet tissue and very little of it. Remember that everything that's deposited into a marine head must quickly move through a hose that's about 1 inch in diameter. It doesn't take much to clog up the works. A small tampon can do wonders—and the repair won't be enjoyable for anyone.

Many boaters place a sign in their heads, all of which warn of dire consequences for those who make unnecessary deposits there. One of the most popular signs reads, "Don't put anything into the head unless you have eaten it first"—a bit gross, but effective. Take the time to teach guests to operate the head, and remember that it can be very intimidating to first timers. I have had some folks refuse beverages for an entire day to avoid having to use the head. Demonstrate the correct amount of toilet paper to use by ripping off two sheets. If they use more, they'll feel guilt ridden. Leaving these issues to guesswork will only mean problems.

When alongside a dock, make use of the marina's restroom facilities (which are also called the head), whenever possible, and encourage your crew to do the same. The walk will feel good and the holding tank won't need to be emptied as often. A marine toilet is a very complex device; treat it kindly so it will be there for you when you really need it.

TYPES OF HEADS

The Basic Models

The most elementary type head is the bucket, commonly used as an all-purpose container on small runabout powerboats and sailing vessels. The advantage of using a bucket is that there is no backlog waste matter to deal with. You simply dump the contents (raw sewage) overboard while no one is looking and you're done. Or, you can save it for the grand flush in a marina toilet once you dock. Women are the most common bucket users. If your boat is large enough to sleep aboard, however, you should not have to be subject to using a bucket as a toilet.

A vessel large enough to have a galley and sleeping accommodations will be equipped with either a portable potty or a built-in holding tank. Both types allow you to store waste products in a holding tank (which never seems to be large enough). The tank mixture is seasoned with "blue stuff" to disintegrate, neutralize, and deodorize waste until it can be pumped out at a later time.

Holding tanks need to be unloaded frequently or your boat will emit a stench rendering it unapproachable. The holding capacity and sophistication of these tanks increase relative to the size of the boat.

Catch-and-Carry Heads

A portable marine toilet is equipped with a handle so you can pick the holding tank up like a suitcase and casually saunter your wares ashore for proper dumping. I have yet to find one that didn't leak, even if just a little. Portable potties need to be primed with a gallon or two of water and some of that same blue disintegrator that's used in holding tanks. Read the directions that come with your toilet for information about the proper amounts to use. Locate the disposal area at a marina when it is time to empty it, rinse it out with a hose, and you are back in business with a fresh, clean toilet.

If your captain is clever, like mine, he may develop a more convenient means of dumping the contents of your portable potty. On our first boat, he got tired of dragging our portable potty out of its little niche in our head and up to the disposal area, so he rigged a hose and pump contraption between the forward head and the stern of our boat. This enabled us to pump out our head while at sea, just like the big boats do. This device, which took three of us to man, worked most of the time. Every so often, though, a section of the hose dropped off midpumping and we ended up mopping odiferous blue-green ooze off our berth.

Built-in Holding Tanks

Once you have operated with a portable potty for a while, your yen for the convenience of a built-in holding tank will become an obsession. The larger the tank, the longer you will be able to wait before it will need to be pumped out. Holding tanks work on the fill and flush theory. Seawater is pumped in to flush the waste out of the toilet bowl and wash it into the holding tank. The most common method for emptying a holding tank is to pump out the head while in deep water a good distance from civilization. Never, never, never pump out your head at a mooring or dock area. Your neighbors will find you and bar you from the all future dock parties. They will know who you are by just following their noses. If you are desperate and cannot take the boat away from shore for dumping, hire a pump-out service to come to your boat and do it for you.

Electric Heads

The most sophisticated marine head I have encountered is one that's powered from a boat's batteries, generator, or dockside electricity. When I first found out the toilet on our new boat would be electric, I was thrilled. I had visions of a flush toilet like we use at home—but then I realized that wouldn't be considered electric. An electric head is just like a standard marine toilet in that it has a holding tank and still must be flushed and pumped. The difference is that, instead of a person having to move the pump handle up and down, the process is done electrically. In action, it looks quite comical.

One pull of a small silver button gets the pumping process going; push it in and the process stops. One problem on our boat is that we have two silver buttons, one of which is the pump-out button. We have had to be very specific about instructing guests as to which silver button they must pull to flush the toilet. Should you ever use an electric head, know that you must push the button in to shut the pump off when you are through; otherwise, the motor will wear out and you will risk flooding the boat.

MAINTAINING A BOAT'S HEAD

There are all kinds of commercial products available to help keep head odor down, disintegrate the waste, and to lubricate and maintain it so it will function properly. Let's start with the blue stuff, which is the mariners' nickname for the substance that is poured into a head to refresh it after it's been pumped out. The original product for this job was blue, but now green and colorless products have surfaced. In my experience, all-natural products are not as effective as traditional head treatments. The stronger the better.

The marine toilet is a complicated species—just look at a parts replacement kit. It contains a mountain of gaskets and connectors that contribute to its smooth operation, so be careful what you use when you clean and lubricate a marine toilet. The average marine head cannot tolerate the same heavy cleaners you use in your toilets at home. Stay away from products that contain chlorine, formaldehyde, or pine oil—they will dry out a head's delicate hoses and connectors over time. Some units carry a "caution" sticker on them. Carefully review the cleaning instructions for your specific head to see what is recommended. When in doubt, use only mild cleaners.

While chartering a sailboat in the Islands, we learned some tricks for pampering marine heads. Now, every few days that we're aboard, we flush a squirt or two of dish detergent through the head and follow it with one or two capfuls of vegetable oil. Both items are standard galley supplies and will keep a head clean and lubricated, while being kind to the environment. The oil makes a big difference in the ease of flushing the head—the workings will glide instead of groan.

If you boat in salt water, it is not unusual for calcium deposits to build up in the valves and hoses connected to a head. To prevent serious calcium buildup and potential problems, flush a half cup or so of white vinegar through the head about once a month. Before you close up the boat to go home, swish a bit of disinfectant around the bowl and the seat to sanitize and deodorize the head and refresh it for your next visit.

SURVIVING PUMP-OUT SERVICE

If an unpleasant odor begins to emanate from the head on your boat, or if it seems harder to flush, the head is probably suffering from the pressure of being full—a sure sign of trouble. Your choices are to take the boat out for a spin and rid yourself of the foul stuff or call the local pump-out service. Most services monitor a marine radio channel. Many marinas offer pump-out as a free service because, as incredulous as it may seem, there are boaters who will actually pump the contents of their head into the waters around their slip, usually after dark. At any cost, hiring a pump-out service is worth it.

Understand that the job of the service is limited to the actual pump-out, and any cleanup afterwards is all yours. You need to be on your toes for this chore. Have the hose ready and get out of the way. Built-up pressure may result in an indignant outburst from your waste valve as it belches its messy sigh of relief. If you can locate a pressure release valve somewhere in the fittings of your head (my captain swears our boat doesn't have one), release it before opening the outside valve.

Also, make sure all nearby hatches and portholes are closed. I suggest surrounding the valve area with a large, tightened trash bag and reaching in with a gloved hand to release the valve. If you are sensible, like we weren't, you won't wait so long to call the pump-out boat (our service was aptly named "Repulsive") and your waste valve will only issue a slight hiss and maybe, just maybe, you'll be home free.

We learned to take these precautions the hard way. Due to a storm, we had been forced to remain on Block Island an extra few days and were nursing a swollen holding tank. We placed a rescue call to the local pump-out service, but never having used one before, we weren't quite certain what to expect. When my husband attempted to open the waste valve for them, brownish-green ick splatted up and out, all over the boat and onto the onlookers. I, safely sheltered down below, silently chuckled until I realized I had left a porthole open. We have been extra cautious with pump-out service ever since.

PART THREE

Food on the Fly

THE OCEAN IS CALM. The captain is relaxed at the helm, letting the wind take your boat wherever it may. You sigh, then roll over to tan your back. There is no peace like that of being on tranquil waters. Then it happens. Hunger strikes and you're on the move. A side effect of sailing is a growling stomach. My mother used to say it was the salt air. Simple foods, fast foods, fancy foods, your crew won't be fussy. When on the boat, they will eat almost anything.

Your galley may be as primitive as a portable stove, a cooler, a jug of water, and a bucket, or as elegant as a fancy cruise liner's. It doesn't matter. If you like to sleep aboard your boat, some basic food supplies will stave off hunger and heighten your enjoyment of your time aboard. It's okay to take it easy. Get your galley set up. Then relax and enjoy anything from lunch under way to a romantic after-sail dinner. Your choice.

CHAPTER

10

What Do You Need?

OUTFITTING A GALLEY

What kind of cook are you? Will you give the captain some burgers to throw on the grill, add a bag of chips, some raw baby carrots and pickles, and call it dinner? Is a cold sandwich acceptable meal fare? Or, will you delight in using all the tiny facilities aboard to produce the type of meal you might cook at home? We are all different. One of the things that's so wonderful about boating is that it frees us to pursue our personal style. If you are a gourmet cook at home, you might enjoy taking a vacation from cooking and find a restaurant; then again, you may enjoy the challenges of creating a specialty pasta dish aboard. Your cooking profile will define the type and amount of cooking supplies you will need to furnish your galley.

DINNERWARE

Let's start at the back and move forward. What will you eat your meals on? Your options vary from disposable dinnerware to real ceramic or china dishes. The elegance and style of the dinnerware you select will depend on the answers to these questions:

- How much time are you willing to spend on cleanup?
- Will you have enough water to spare for dishwashing?
- Where and how will you be traveling?
- What are your personal preferences?
- How much do you want to impress your guests?

Disposable Dinnerware

Paper plates, paper or plastic cups, and plastic utensils are tops when it comes to boaters' preferred diningware attire. No self-respecting boater minds eating on paper, and cleanup is a snap. You eliminate the fuss of trying to degrease dirty dishes with cold water, are able to quickly clear clutter, and easily remove food odors from the boat. If you are serving hot or wet food on paper plates, choose a firm plate that will not cave in or soak through, or reinforce thin plates by setting them on reusable rattan or plastic plate holders. Although inexpensive, disposable plastic bowls and dishes make sensible serving bowls for gooey and greasy foods, I tend to avoid using too many of them because they are not recyclable.

SHE SAID: *"Look, no dishes!"*

HE SAID: *"How can four people generate so much trash in two days?"*

Plastic or paper drink cups are a godsend. With no dish-washer, keeping up with clean glasses can be a real chore. You can drink through a package a day if you have kids or are constantly offering iced beverages to your friends and neighbors. I mount stick-up holders filled with two-ounce paper cups in both the head and the galley. (Used cups are handy to leave in the head to contain tiny bits of trash like dental floss and used tissues until I can toss them into the trash.) Plastic knives, forks, and spoons work fine until your dinners escalate from hot dogs and hamburgers to food that needs to be pierced or sliced. If you are on the move for several days, using lots of paper plates and cups may overload your trash can. Nevertheless, one of the most inconvenient problems you will encounter with disposable dinnerware is running out of it.

The Good Stuff

If you are spending a respectable amount of time on board, substantial dinnerware is a practical complement to paper and plastic disposable dinnerware. It's nice to use a fork that doesn't break when you stab a piece of meat or to eat from a plate that doesn't leak grease stains onto your shorts. A nice heavy mug for a morning cup of coffee beats a foam or paper cup, hands down. Paper goods are like sleeping bags. Boaters and campers almost always start out using them, but they eventually crave something better, like *real* dinnerware or *real* sheets and blankets.

Anyone will agree that ceramic dishes, mugs, serving bowls, and glasses are nice to use, but how practical are they on a boat? I'll start by getting on my soapbox and repeating my aversion to keeping breakable items on board, particularly on a sailboat. My primary concerns are locating a safe spot for them and risking injuries from broken pottery or glass.

The type of boat you have and its ability to house fragile objects will affect your decision. The steadier, more predictable motion of a powerboat is kinder to fragile items than the often erratic movements of a boat under sail. We met a couple that was living aboard a 45-foot sailboat, one identical to ours, and the wife was kind enough to give me a tour. It is always interesting to note how other boaters use their storage areas. I was completely stunned when she opened a cabinet to display a set of delicate, fine china. And these people have sailed all over the world!

Maybe I'm just a pessimist, but I feel that if you keep real dishes and glasses aboard you will need to guard them like they are your grandchildren. Allocate a secure storage spot where they will not knock into each other or fall over, and don't leave them stacked in the dish drain when you are under way.

You can acquire safe, unbreakable dinnerware in two ways: expensively and cheaply. With either option you can get the same attractive functionality—it just depends on how much you are willing to spend. It is doubtful anyone except you will notice the difference between marine dinnerware and plastic plates, although one important advantage of marine dinnerware is that plates, bowls, and cups have rubber rings on the undersides to help them stay put. The other benefit is that it is practically indestructible, unless you decide to fry eggs on it in your oven or microwave. It is only mildly heat resistant.

Choosing marine dinnerware is like picking out good china for your home. It comes in many pretty patterns and you can purchase it by the place setting or open stock. Select a pattern you love because you will have it a long time. I've used my set for 12 years and, other than a few scratches and an occasional rubber ring that's needed to be reset, it is still in nearly perfect condition. My pattern is still being made and I have added to it over the years. A recent marine catalog listed these prices for open-stock, nonskid items: $4.50 for a mug; $10.25 for a 10-inch dinner plate; $5.95 for a matching insulated glass; and $21.95 for a set of four plastic wine glasses.

A colorful set of inexpensive plastic dinnerware will give you the same feeling of stability as marine dinnerware when you dine and there's always a sale on them somewhere. Look for soup bowls and mugs that hold hot liquids without cracking and leaking. If cups and glasses are non-breakable and stackable, they won't shatter when they topple over, and will store easily. With the popularity of sports drinks there are an increasing variety of spill-proof, insulated drink containers available. Look in the picnic goods departments for tall colorful glasses for iced drinks and stemware for wine. Wide-bottomed, heavy, plastic or stainless steel mugs with sipping lids keep coffee hot and confined while under way—and they work beautifully for cold drinks as well. Often you can purchase various sizes of rubber banding that will slip around the base of an ordinary glass, cup, or jar to make it nonslip.

To make your new dinnerware nonslip, glue circles of rubber mesh on the bottom. This method can also be used to convert platters, serving bowls, vases, pitchers, pet food bowls, candlesticks, portable CDs, tape decks, and anything else you are worried about. The procedure is simple.

Purchase one roll of rubber mesh. You can find it almost anywhere and it comes in decorator colors.

Trace the base of the item onto a piece of paper to make a pattern, then use it to cut the proper shape from the rubber mesh.

Use waterproof glue to permanently bond the rubber mesh to the plastic. Avoid using your fingers to tap the rubber in place—use a stick or the backside of a utensil instead. Keep glue remover handy.

Allow the item to dry completely, upside down.

FLATWARE

You won't impress anyone with tarnished black flatware, so I recommend leaving sterling silver flatware at home. Typical boating flatware, with its distinctive red-, blue-, green-, or white-colored handles, is made of stainless steel because it is one of the few metals that can survive the salt air. Don't bother buying the pretty stand that some of these sets are displayed on—they are perfectly useless and are a nuisance to store.

During my first year of boating, I bought a new set of kitchen flatware for my home and relegated my old one to the boat. When we upgraded from our Buccaneer 27, Captain *My Way* insisted we get proper nautical flatware, hence the white-handled set we now own. I bought my first set from a marine store and it was *not* cheap. I have since added to it by keeping an eye out for bargains at discount stores. They just won't wear out. But you know, I would trade my nautical set anytime for simple old flatware that stacks flatter and takes less space in my silverware drawers, anytime.

A basic dinnerware set for four people might include four each of the following: dinner plates, luncheon plates, small soup bowls, cups or mugs, plastic glasses, stainless forks, stainless teaspoons, and serrated steak knives. I'd add to that two serving spoons (one slotted), one serving fork, and one platter.

The disposable serving pieces that I keep on board include paper plates and bowls; paper or plastic cups; insulated paper or Styrofoam cups; plastic forks, knives, and spoons; and paper napkins.

CONTAINERS AND ACCESSORIES

Let items do double duty. Plastic airtight containers can both store and serve food. I love straw baskets. I can put food, like chips or bread, into them directly, after first lining them with a paper napkin or an attractive dishtowel. They are also fantastic for serving wrapped sandwiches when under way; and they happily hold paper plates, knives, forks, napkins, salt, and pepper for a meal in the cockpit or keep the catsup, mustard, and relish for a cookout. What I love most about baskets is they don't need to be washed (even though they can be if necessary), and they come in all sizes and shapes. I use my flat-bottomed, straight-sided, rectangular basket the most because it holds more and keeps items upright. Small baskets make good space dividers in cabinets and are wonderful for grouping tiny items, like spices, toiletries, or the captain's collection of screws.

Another all-purpose container that I can't do without is a disposable aluminum foil pan. I keep several on hand in various sizes. They are inexpensive, handy for controlling sloppy foods, and work well for oven warming and baking. They also make a great meat or fish holder for trips between the galley and the barbecue grill. When they get messy, just throw them away and bring on the replacements.

You will want to add or subtract to this suggested starter list, according to your cooking style.

- Plastic serving bowl with cover
- Plastic storage containers
- Rubberized or plastic drink pitcher
- Baskets
- Thermos bottle
- Can opener

- Corkscrew
- Ice pick
- Aluminum foil
- Disposable foil baking pans
- Resealable plastic bags, assorted sizes
- Trash bags

COOKWARE

Now that you've got something to eat on, what will you cook with? How will you heat a can of soup, fry some eggs, or make toast and coffee? Will you need a large pot to boil lobsters? Will you want to bake cookies? You will find that the bulk of your onboard cooking can be accomplished in very few pots. As always, consider where you will store your cookware before you lug every pan in your kitchen to the boat. Get started with a few pans from home you can spare.

Keep in mind that all cookware should fit on your stove top. If pans are too large for a burner, your food will be half cooked. Also, if you plan to cook when the boat is moving, whether it is a rough day on a mooring or you are under sail, cooking pans must be anchored down with clamps, called fiddles, on the stove, to keep them from taking a ride of their own.

Aluminum will corrode in salt air, so choose stainless steel or enamel cookware, and preferably nonstick. The better the quality of the pan, the easier it will be to cook with and to clean afterward. Cheap pans heat unevenly and, as it is, you will be using an erratic heat source. If you are purchasing a new set of pans, stainless steel, stackable pans with removable handles are a good option for ever-tight pan lockers. An eight-piece set costs approximately $350 and stores in less than one cubic foot of space. Boat designers barely leave room to house a coffee pot in most galleys, let alone a full set of pans, so these may be a worthwhile investment for you. If you have commandeered a nice lower locker for your cookware, you may have the space for a more traditional set.

Many offshore cooks rely on pressure cookers to quickly cook stews, steam vegetables, and prepare other dishes. If you have an old one kicking around your basement, your boat is a practical place to make good use of it because it cuts cooking time and pot hovering, leaving you free to join the group for cocktails while your dinner is simmering. A pressure cooker also uses less of your precious water than conventional cooking methods, reduces galley heat, and doubles as a spill-proof serving pan. I am told that the new pressure cookers are very safe, marine approved, and guaranteed not to blow a hole through the roof of your boat. Prices range from $95 to $130.

With a nonstick, 10-inch skillet you will be able to turn out a variety of breakfast foods—pancakes, French toast, eggs—or quickly sauté a meal on the night your barbecue gets rained out. A medium-size saucepan with a cover heats up anything from soup and spaghetti sauce to tea water.

If instant coffee offends you, buy a stainless steel percolator like the old-fashioned type your mother used before the advent of the electric coffee maker. You will have to scout kitchen shops because nonelectric pots are scarce, and then re-educate yourself on how to use them. But it will be worth all your trouble just to have the smell of real coffee wafting through your boat.

I keep a baking pan aboard for transporting fish or meat for the grill or baking a birthday cake. A foil pan works as well as a metal one for most purposes and can be thrown away once it's too messy to bother washing. To save pan storage space you can substitute foil cups, or foil cupcake liners, for cupcake tins. Just set them in your baking pan, fill, and bake away.

If you like lobster, steamers, and other shellfish you are liable to come across while sailing, or simply enjoy cooking pasta for a crowd, find a spot to store a large pot on your boat. An outdoor locker will work fine if you place the pot in a plastic bag to keep it clean. Don't skimp on size—an 8- to 12-quart covered pot is good. The pot can go on the charcoal grill, the stove top, and can work as a stew or saucepot. Take advantage of the empty storage space it provides when not being used—fill its cavity with supplies, such as extra paper plates, cups, and dishtowels. A large pot also makes a good sink for washing dishes.

Those of us who have dockside power outlets find electric fry pans indispensable. They can be used anywhere there is a 110-volt AC outlet. If you can find an old set of directions for yours, you will remember that an electric fry pan can be used like an oven for baking. Place a wire rack in the bottom of the pan, preheat it to the desired baking temperature, and then place the casserole or cake pan on the rack. Cover the pan and time bake cycles as if you were cooking in an oven. I used to bake in my electric fry pan years ago when I didn't have an air conditioned kitchen. It's amazing how resourceful you can be if you give it some thought. This pan makes a great steamer for clams and is large enough to hold enough cutlets, stew, or pasta sauce for four to eight people. When you use an electric fry pan, make sure to secure it in a nonslip area. Boats move, even when at dock.

My basic pan wardrobe consists of the following:
12-quart stockpot and cover
10-inch fry pan with cover
1-quart saucepan with cover

Additional cookware that's nice to have:
Pressure cooker
Electric fry pan

Stainless steel coffee or tea pot
Marine toaster
8- x 8- x 2-inch nonstick metal or foil baking pan

Other basic cooking equipment:
Barbecue grill
Metal or plastic spatula for skillet cooking
Wooden spoons
Rubber scraper
Colander
Nesting stainless steel or plastic mixing bowls with covers
Measuring cups and spoons
Potholders/oven mitts
Long-handled barbecue fork and spatula
Paper towels
Pre-moistened towellettes
Waterproof matches

CHAPTER

11

What Will You Cook?

FIRST, THE BASICS

Fast food is the credo of most recreational boaters. On a gorgeous day, no sane person would want to spend hours trapped in a small galley preparing a meal. If you prowl the supermarkets and food warehouses, you'll find a glut of convenience foods. Buy packaged dinner mixes, prepared pasta sauces, rice dishes, baking mixes, and drink mixes. Enhance them by adding meat, vegetables, and some water, milk, or broth.

Processed foods you wouldn't think of serving at home become gala meals when presented in a cockpit on a starry night. Cook some pasta and top it with bottled sauce. Voilà! Dinner for two or 12 people, none of whom will miss the bread and salad if you give them enough wine. On raw, rainy days, bake a cake and fill the boat with the aroma of vanilla. No matter how poorly it comes out, everyone will rave over it. It's amazing how something you wouldn't think of as fine dining at home takes on an ambiance befitting chateaubriand when served on a boat.

Should you venture to actually cook aboard, never forget that your boat is likely to move—and often just when you least expect it. To prevent spills, make certain that pots and other cooking equipment are securely clamped down on the stove, don't fill pots more than halfway, and use the sink to contain cooking items so they will not jostle about. To keep pots from sliding and to protect countertops, set them on folded, damp towels or rubber mats.

Whenever possible, mix and cook in the same pan to reduce pan handling and dishwashing. Use heavy duty, resealable plastic bags or empty cans and bottles to mix batters, marinades, and salad dressings, rather than dirty a bowl. And, clean up as you go—there's no room to store messes.

Avoid the common mistake of having too much food by planning your menu before each stay and bringing only what you will realistically use. But don't get too stringent. On one of our first boating excursions, I tried a little too hard to economize space. I actually counted out the slices of bread we would require for four or five days of sandwiches, and that's all I brought. It totaled a single loaf of bread. By the middle of the week, we were eating stale bread speckled with telltale white spots, which I now know wasn't flour, but mold. Lunchtime was not pleasant on our boat that week.

It's hard to store warm leftovers on a boat, so select portion sizes that will feed the crowd *once*. If you plan to use your own recipes, pre-measure and pre-mix ingredients at home and seal them in plastic bags. Freeze liquids and sauces in bags, also, and then use the bags as ice packs until they defrost and you are ready to use them. Plan to do as little mixing as possible in the galley. Counter space is usually tight and may even be nonexistent, so it will be difficult to juggle bowls and pans to create the masterpiece you want to deliver for dinner.

Think about the meals you enjoy at home. If you can cook it on a stove top in your kitchen, you can cook it in your galley. You may even wish to bring a cookbook or two. All it takes is some planning. Keep your boat stocked with small amounts of the seasonings you commonly use at home, then bring to the boat the extra items you will need to prepare your onboard menus. Apportion fresh meats, seafood, breads, fruits, and vegetables so you will have enough for your trip. And most importantly, don't spend too much time in the galley. You are not there to cook, you are there to sail.

ONBOARD STAPLES

If you take your boat away for overnight excursions, it is essential to keep a few emergency rations so you and your loved ones won't end up dining on potato chips and diet coke if your destination plans are upset. You'll be glad you thought ahead when a simple three-hour trip takes six and you aren't able to get to the restaurant you'd planned on for dinner, or when friends you had planned on meeting for a cookout at a remote harbor don't show up—and they were bringing the food.

Staples can save you in such instances. Dinty Moore's Beef Stew and brown bread is one of the standby meals experienced boaters rely upon. Don't ask me why. It certainly isn't a dinner I would serve at home, but on the water, especially after having fought through a miserably cold rainy day, the combination can taste like a gourmet meal. Simply open up the cans and figure out a way to warm the stew. If you can boil water, you can heat the stew by setting the can in hot water for about 10 minutes, or until it is heated. Stir occasionally. And in case you're not from New England, let me introduce you to brown bread. It is canned bread that actually tastes pretty good. I like the kind with raisins. You'll find it with the beans and stews at grocery stores. (See chapter 12 for ideas on using leftover brown bread.)

I've learned the hard way how to be creative with just a few staples.

- If the lunchmeat has spoiled, open a can of tuna and make tuna salad.
- Keep your favorite pre-mixed baking mix on hand to bake biscuits when you are low on bread, and to make pancakes. Keep a supply of canned or boxed lunch and dinner items; a large jar of pasta sauce and a pound of linguini can save your skin when unexpected company stays on or when the weather is so miserable that all you want to do is cozy up in the boat with a bottle of wine and a hot filling meal.
- For last-minute hors d'oeuvres, try canned, smoked oysters and crackers or just set out a can of nuts or a bag of chips.

People aren't fussy on a boat, so dip into those emergency rations and let your creativity run amok.

Some staples are very practical to keep aboard because they have uses other than for cooking. I use vegetable oil for everything, even salad dressing, and no one notices it's not olive oil if they don't see me making it. Vegetable oil is also a safe lubricant for plastic, fiberglass, or metal moving parts. I not only cook with white vinegar, I use it to clean lots of boat surfaces. Lemon or lime juice in those little plastic containers are compact to store and a delightful way to perk up a tired fish or chicken dish. They're also good for degreasing and deodorizing sticky cooking hands. I always keep fresh limes aboard for the captain's rum cokes, so there is always an extra wedge to squeeze. I have come to enjoy my lobster with a squeeze of lime instead of butter—it's lower in calories and I don't have to fuss with the mess of melted butter.

Baking soda is astonishing. I use it for everything *except* cooking on board. It deodorizes and gently cleans an ice chest; it removes stains that form inside the toilet bowl and on stainless steel oven tops, sinks, and countertops; and it is gentler and less abrasive than a commercial cleanser. Mix equal parts of baking soda and white vinegar to remove stains on carpets and upholstered cushions. (I learned this trick from treating pet mishaps at home.)

Remember to keep a running list of the items you use up so you can replenish them.

Here's my leave-aboard-for-the-season list (you will want to make up your own):

- Seasonings: salt and pepper, basil, oregano, garlic and any other favorites or seasoning mixes
- 1 head of garlic
- 1 piece of fresh ginger
- Vegetable oil
- Vinegar
- Baking soda
- Cajun seasoning
- Small, unopened jars or individual packets of catsup, mustard, and mayonnaise
- Barbecue sauce, soy sauce, any other favorites
- Coffee, coffee filters, tea bags, hot chocolate packets
- Packaged drink mixes or concentrates
- Sugar packets
- Nondairy creamer packets
- Canned or dried soup mixes
- Canned tuna, shrimp, or crab meat
- Prepared spaghetti sauce (1 large jar)

○ One-pound package spaghetti
○ Large can beef or chicken stew
○ 1 can brown bread
○ 1 can baked beans
○ 1 can pineapple, mandarin oranges, or other fruit
○ 1 package brownie mix
○ Small box buttermilk baking mix
○ Maple syrup
○ Boxed, canned milk (such as Parmalat)
○ Peanut butter
○ Cookies and crackers, including a box of ginger cookies and
     plain crackers (for queasy tummies)
○ Potato and tortilla chips
○ Salsa and/or bean dip
○ Canned nuts
○ Canned smoked oysters

SHOPPING FOR FOODS THAT STORE WELL

Food supplies that you select for your boat must meet certain criteria to withstand the rigors of time, temperature, and humidity. Whenever possible, it's best to store foods in their nonperishable states, in packages that take as little space as possible. For items that must be refrigerated after opening, such as mayonnaise or catsup, keep on the boat a supply of unopened jars. Once they are opened, unless you have a reliable boat refrigerator, you will need to shuttle them between the boat and your home refrigerator to keep them fresh. Check restaurant supply and warehouse food stores for one-serving size packets of condiments that do not require refrigeration, which can be safely left on your boat all season. If you are making lots of sandwiches, using one-serving packets is a nuisance. They are time-consuming to open and the empties are pesky to get rid of.

Cake frosting, muffin and brownie mixes are available at supermarkets in foil-lined, air- and moisture-proof packets that will last from season to season. I buy sugar and coffee creamers in indi-

vidual packets and put some in a small serving basket, then store
the rest in resealable plastic bags. Keep sugar and flour fresh by enclosing them in plastic bags or containers. Serve individual cereals
right out of their packages. Did you know that the small snack
boxes are scored at the back? Slit open the box along the dotted indicator lines and you've got a dish! Add milk and chow down. I
remember doing this as a kid. Perhaps even better, I recently noticed a prepackaged cereal and milk breakfast in the supermarket
dairy case.

There are several varieties of nonperishable milk alternatives.
Long-life milk, such as Parmalat, which is popular in the islands,
makes a good substitute for fresh milk if you don't mind the
canned taste. I keep a small box of dry milk aboard, reconstitute it
by adding water, and use it for cooking or to supplement fresh
milk. I used to do this several years ago to save money. I mixed
one-part reconstituted dry milk to one-part fresh milk; if the jug
was well shaken and cold, my kids never noticed the difference.

Powdered drink mixes are a blessing if you've got kids on
board. Iced tea, lemonade, and other flavored drink mixes come in
small packets, last forever, and can be quickly reconstituted with
the mere tilt of a jug of water.

To add zest to convenience foods, buy a few sample sizes of
special sauces, exotic mustards, and salad dressings—they can
dramatically decrease your time in the galley without sacrificing
flavor. I prefer to mix my own salad dressings, so I keep vinegar
and oil aboard (neither needs refrigeration) to use as a base. I add
a few spices to the oil to brush on fish, skinless chicken, and vegetables that we grill. A friend of mine who is a gourmet boat cook
repackages all her dry goods and spices into neatly labeled resealable plastic bags. They take very little space and can be
grouped in plastic storage boxes to further protect them. Another
friend relies on several specialty sauces to easily produce dishes
with her special flare.

Once I open a box of cereal or crackers, or a package of chips,
I put the leftovers, box or bag and all, in a resealable plastic bag so
they will remain fresh—they'll last from week to week if stored
airtight.

When you are leaving nonperishable dry foods, such as baking mixes, pasta, and potato chips aboard for long periods of time,

including over the winter, protect them against mold, mildew, and mites by removing the contents from any cardboard packaging and sealing them in large plastic bags or covered containers. Cardboard attracts roaches and other undesirables, so it is essential to remove foods from their outer cardboard cartons.

PROTECTING PERISHABLE FOODS

Man cannot live on cans (of food) alone. No matter how hard you try to make do without perishables, you will still want to have fresh fruits and vegetables, dairy products, meats, seafood, and breads on board to satisfy your palates. These are staples you will typically buy at the market or bring from home for each trip. (See chapter 1 for my list of "can't do without" perishable foods.)

Milk

For a stay on the boat, bring the same amount of fresh milk you would normally consume at home. Place small amounts in seal-tight plastic jugs or bring quarts, half-gallons, or gallons of milk in their original containers. If paper beverage containers leak once they are opened, reseal the opening with a piece of waterproof tape or transfer the contents into a plastic jug. Store large bottles upright at the bottom of the cooler or ice chest.

Seafood and Meats

It is important to keep seafood and meat very cold. Whenever possible, use seafood the same day you buy it—even if it means making a special stop for it on the way to the boat or getting in the car on a Saturday afternoon and heading to the fish store. If you must purchase fish in advance, wrap it tightly in foil and store it in a plastic bag. Rinse fish and pat it dry before preparing it for cooking. If there's a slightly fishy odor when you open it, although the fish may not be as fresh as you would like, it is probably still edible. Apply a healthy squeeze of lemon or a dollop of a flavorful sauce and hope no one notices. Worse case, you'll be dining out.

Bring dinner meats, such as steaks and hamburger, to the boat in their frozen state unless you plan to use them on the day of your arrival. I find it is especially important to double wrap meats because, as they defrost, the juices tend to drip—and it's a real mess to clean up. Luncheon meats from the deli are usually very fresh and won't keep as long as meats that are more solid. Keep deli meats grouped and protected by storing them in rectangular plastic containers or a resealable plastic bag. Remember that food spoils more quickly when stored in an ice chest or cooler than in a refrigerator because the temperatures are less consistent. Therefore, it's important to use meats, like roast beef and turkey, as soon as possible. I find that deli ham lasts the longest and is also the most versatile of lunchmeats. I brown it in a bit of butter and serve it for breakfast instead of bacon with eggs or pancakes, as well as use it for sandwiches.

Bread

I always include a loaf of sliced bread as part of my bread supply for a trip because, like ham, it can be used as a basis for dishes other than sandwiches. Think of making French toast or buttered toast and jam for breakfast fare, and croutons for your evening salad. Although it's tempting to buy fresh bakery bread, it goes stale quickly. So, unless you will be using it within a day or so, opt for breads made with preservatives. They will stay fresh and will be resistant to mold.

Wrap any bread you don't expect to use soon in foil or plastic and store it in a cool, open area or find a dry spot for it in your cooler or ice chest. I've read that it is possible to preserve bread for long periods of time by wiping the loaf with vinegar (yet another use for vinegar), then wrapping it tightly in foil or plastic wrap. I haven't been destitute enough to test this theory, but I can't help but wonder what marinated bread tastes like.

A hanging net hammock makes a safe, out-of-the-way place to stow bread without crushing it. I always seem to have a large quantity of breads when the kids come to the boat for the weekend and find that if I put the soft rolls and loaves in my overhead galley hammock and cushion them with puffy chip bags, they will retain their shapes.

Pita bread is adaptable and less of a hassle to store than fluffy yeast breads and rolls because it lays flat and keeps longer than traditional bread.

Eggs

It is safe to store eggs without refrigeration for about three weeks if the weather is cool. Farm fresh eggs that have not previously been refrigerated keep the longest. Wash eggs to remove external bacteria, and then coat them lightly with a film of petroleum jelly to seal the pores and protect them from bacteria. Eggs preserved in this way should be good for a month or two without refrigeration. This trick is especially handy if you don't use eggs frequently, yet wish to have an occasional one aboard to use for baking a birthday cake. I always keep an "emergency" egg prepared like this in a plastic container in my galley cupboard.

You can bring eggs to the boat by the dozen. They will be safe in their original cartons as long as they are kept level, secure, and uncrunched. Plastic egg holders that latch shut, which are available at camping and marine stores, do a good job of protecting eggs from breaking. They are also convenient for crowded storage areas because the holder can be tipped and stored in multiple positions. To determine if an egg is still fresh and safe to consume, place it in a pan of water. If it floats, it's bad, so toss it out!

Fruit

Don't forgo bringing delicious summer peaches and plums aboard because it's hard to find a place to put them where they won't get bruised. Invest in a tiered, hanging mesh basket and hang it in your galley. These baskets are inexpensive and available in enough bright colors to match any decor. Fill the basket with fruits and vegetables and let it sway when you sail. You'll no longer have to worry about delicate fruit banging around in coolers or rolling around on countertops.

Keep in mind that fruit doesn't keep any better on a boat than it does at home. If left out for very long it will attract fruit flies, which in a confined area can drive you nutty. Placing fruit in the cooler or ice chest will reduce this problem. If it is the kind that bruises easily, protect it by putting it in covered plastic containers. Limit the amount of fruits you bring to the boat to that which you can realistically consume.

Garlic

If you frequently cook with fresh garlic, buy a head and leave it aboard. Garlic will keep for several weeks if stored loose and in open air. (It will also keep the werewolves away.) If you use garlic infrequently, you are better off buying a small jar of dehydrated garlic or enclosing a few tablespoons of it in a small plastic bag, and keeping it stored aboard with your other seasonings. Fresh gingerroot also keeps without refrigeration and is a practical item to have on hand.

WATER ALL AROUND AND NOT A DROP TO DRINK

A taste test of the tap water on your boat may be a real turnoff. Although boat dealers will tell you that there is no reason why you can't drink the water that's stored in your tanks—and that's true, it may indeed be potable—it can taste so bad it will make the insides of your mouth pucker. Many factors affect the taste of tank water on a boat. Yours may taste just fine, but most boat water, even after scrupulous tank cleaning and water purifying, is likely to have an off taste. This is especially true if the drinking water at your marina is city water loaded with chemicals. Do your own test by ordering a glass of water at a local restaurant. If the water doesn't taste good there, how much better can it get after it funnels through a hose and into your boat's water tanks, and then sits there for an extended period of time?

Tasty drinking water is hard to get unless it's bottled, which is why many boaters lug gallon jugs of water—enough for drinking as well as cooking—to their boats each weekend. (Off-tasting water makes yucky coffee, yucky soup, and yucky pasta.) That's a lot of extra baggage to add to your already gargantuan load, not to mention the problem of finding a secure, accessible storage spot for the jugs while under way. A lower locker, or even the bilge, may be a safe spot to tuck them away, but be aware that plastic jugs may leak under pressure, so keep them upright and avoid jamming them into tight spots.

So what can you do to assure adequate, tasty water for satisfying drinking, cooking, and other oral needs? Here are some options:

For drinking water and small cooking projects, keep a portable, pitcher-type water filter filled with drinking water in your cooler, and refill as needed. Water purifiers are also available in individual sizes. Stand-alone water filters can be purchased from $20 to $200, but know that they can be bulky to store.

Keep a supply of two unopened gallons of bottled water stowed aboard for cooking or emergency drinking. Make space in a locker or in your bilge, where the water will drain out if they leak.

Beg the captain to install a good water filter on the galley sink. We discovered one at a boat show that wasn't too expensive and it has permanently eliminated our need to lug jugs and waste valuable storage space. We change the filter once a year and have moved it from boat to boat as we've upgraded.

Quenching Your Thirst

Our family got tired of drinking soda, so I switched off to iced tea, juices, or just plain water. There are many choices of drink mixes. All you need is good water. I save empty plastic juice containers with screw-on tops to reuse for reconstituting juice or tea mixes—just add water and shake. And when you're through with them, the captain can cut the bottoms off and use them as bailers or for mixing one of his dastardly cleaners.

We also love sun tea. Here's my recipe for it:

Fill a clean, empty plastic juice jug with water. For each 8 ounces of water, add ½ teaspoon of sugar and 1 tea bag, leaving the tab ends of the strings hanging outside the jug. Screw the cap onto the bottle and set it in a snug spot in your cockpit for several hours until the tea turns amber. Serve over ice with a squeeze of lime. This tea will keep un-refrigerated, but won't last long because it will soon be gone.

For many of us, it isn't morning without a cup of coffee. If you're a tea person, skip this section. In addition to jars of instant coffee, you can now buy individual coffee bags that work like tea bags.

These are especially good for boaters who want only an occasional cup of coffee because they store well. Canned coffee is sold with filter packs, and each filter makes a potful. I am a real coffee snob, though. I have mine freshly ground from a local roaster and take it everywhere with me. I even pack a supply when we charter in the islands. To keep it fresh and dry, I seal the original coffee bag in a plastic bag, or pour the coffee into a covered plastic container, depending on the storage space that's available.

If, like me, you are not satisfied with instant, there are many means of producing a fine cup of coffee aboard your boat. My old standby is a stainless steel percolator. It works whether I have an electricity source or not because it only requires a sustained flame. So many of us are used to automatic pots that the art of perking coffee has been long forgotten. I had to learn all over again and can finally produce a perfect pot of perked coffee.

Here's how I make a brewed, eight-cup pot of perked coffee:

Fill the pot with water to the base of the spout. Use one premeasured filter coffee packet, or scoop out 8 tablespoons of coffee that's been ground for a percolator-style pot. I prefer a filter because it is easy to dispose of the grounds and makes cleanup easy. My favorite filter style for a percolator pot is one that's cloverleaf shaped and fits into the base of the coffee basket. It has holes in each corner that slide over the stem of the percolator to enclose the grounds. Put the cover on the pot, light a burner, and bring the coffee to a boil. Once it starts to perk, or bubble up through the glass bulb at the top of the pot, time it for exactly 8 minutes. If you remove the coffee from the fire too soon it will taste like dishwater; too late, it will be bitter.

I recently noticed a 12-volt drip coffeemaker in a boating catalog, but it is easy to prepare drip coffee manually. (I'll bet you forgot about that.) Simply boil water, then pour it through a filter that's packed with your favorite coffee that is set into a thermal container. I experimented with making coffee this way, but went back to the percolator method, because I was never patient enough to wait until the coffee grounds settled before adding more water. So naturally, they overflowed, and I was left with a hot dripping mess to clear away. I don't recommend using a coffee press because it is made of glass, but they are supposed to make excellent coffee and do not require electricity.

If you have an electric power source, you can use the same style electric pot you have at home. If you are planning to purchase an electric drip pot for the boat, consider the thermos carafe style. It's not as delicate as a glass pot, the coffee stays hot without sustained heat, and you can safely bring it into the cockpit for breakfast refills.

CHAPTER

12

Fun with Food

RECIPES FROM MY GALLEY

Lucky you. I like to cook, so I am passing on some simple recipes and suggestions you may wish to try when you are in the mood to play in your galley. Remember that list of staples I suggested? Add some fresh fruits, vegetables, and breads and you will be able to make some wonderful dishes. With cooking capability and a small preparation area, you've got the makings for food on the fly.

LET'S MAKE TOAST

You might not think that toasting is important until the first time you eat cold bagels or plain cold sliced bread for breakfast. The butter doesn't melt and the jelly just sits there, smiling defiantly at you. Mornings on a boat are often cool, and there's nothing like a warm bit of something in your belly to get the day started.

I'll never forget how good hot toast tasted early one miserably rainy morning in Newport, Rhode Island. It was a Sunday and our friends who were aboard with us needed to get back home that day. So, we set sail at the unearthly hour of 6 A.M. despite the conditions, dreading the next six hours we would spend on, and in, the water. The three men (bless them) dressed in full sets of foul-weather regalia and went up to the cockpit to get us under way. The small canvas dodger on *Joy of Summer* afforded them little protection and they were drenched in minutes. Being the "mother" of the ship, I was below making skillet toast when I heard a loud burst of song coming from the cockpit. We may have been dripping wet and uncomfortable that day, but we sure had fun. I guess this wasn't a toast story, after all. The moral is that there is enjoyment in adversity, once you ignore it. We had a liquid type of toast when we arrived home.

You don't have to wait until the heavens dump water on your heads to enjoy toast on your boat. If you have any type of stove top heat source—an ordinary skillet or a stove top marine toaster—you can toast breakfast breads. I use both methods. They work for sliced bread, bagels, English muffins, and almost anything else. I even warm bakery muffins by slicing them in half and lightly toasting both sides.

Stove Top Toasting

There are two models of marine toasters that I am familiar with. Both work like pans on top of a burner and allow you to toast two or four slices of bread at once. With the pyramid-shaped style (which folds flat to store), you can place up to four slices standing slanted on each side, but I find it does not cook as evenly as the rectangular style, in which the toast sits flat down in adjacent sections. Marine toasters work best for making small quantities of toast.

To use a marine toaster, place it over the burner to preheat, but keep the fire low to prevent the bread from scorching. Use a fork or tongs to turn the bread to its second side and remove slices as they are cooked.

For small-to-medium quantities of toast, I use a 10-inch skillet. To make skillet toast, melt and spread about 1 tablespoon of butter or margarine in the bottom of the pan. Place the bread down flat and turn it with a fork as needed. Because it's already buttered, skillet toast comes ready to serve out of the pan. When I'm toasting bagels or English muffins, I place a flat cover or plate over them while they are cut side down in the pan to get them brown and crusty.

Oven Toasting

If you have an oven on your boat, using it to brown or warm breads will save quite a bit of time if you are toasting for a crowd. Use the same method you might at home. Preheat the oven and place the bread on a sheet of aluminum foil. Turn once, then butter and serve. You can also make toast on a barbecue grill. I have a friend who sets a skillet on her grill to cook breakfast eggs. This past year I brought an electric toaster to use when we are dockside, but I find it's easier to brown two bagels in my skillet or marine toaster than it is to unearth the toaster. It is bulky to stow and becomes excess baggage when we travel. If you must have an electric toaster, a toaster oven is more versatile.

Here are some other things you can do with bread, besides making toast.

SEASONED PITA BREAD Slice the bread horizontally and then sprinkle generously with salt, pepper, and your favorite dry spice. Cut into pie-shaped wedges, place them on foil and bake for a few minutes until aromatic. Serve with pesto, hummus dip, or salsa.

LISA MUSUMECI, *Gabriella*, McCurdy & Rhodes 48

GARLIC BREAD (1 loaf) Turn a fresh or failing loaf of French or Italian bread into a treat and serve it as a potato substitute with meat and fish or to complement a spaghetti dinner.

¼ **pound real butter (1 stick)**	1 **tablespoon dried parsley or oregano**
2 **cloves garlic, crushed and minced**	1 **loaf French bread**

Preheat the oven to 400°F. On low heat in a small saucepan, heat together the butter, garlic, and parsley until the butter is just melted. You may also do this in a microwave. Slice the bread in half lengthwise and place on an aluminum foil-lined baking sheet. Brush both sides of the bread with the butter mixture and bake for about 10 minutes, or until the top is browned and bubbling. Cut into wedges and serve hot.

BROWN BREAD This New England staple is so versatile. You can:

Open the can and serve, sliced, with baked beans or stew
Wrap leftovers in foil and make breakfast toast
Make ham and cheese sandwiches for lunch
Spread with cream cheese and slice into bite-sized pieces for appe-
tizers

WHAT DO DO WITH OTHER STAPLES

You probably have some leftovers and other food items on hand
that you'd like to get extra mileage from. Here are some more
recipes.

Canned pineapple can be eaten plain, make blender drinks, or be
added to recipes to enhance their flavor. Here are two of my favorites:

PINEAPPLE TUNA SALAD You can use pineapple to add an interesting twist to a traditional luncheon salad.

> 1 can tuna, drained
> 1 small can pineapple tidbits, drained well
> 1 to 2 tablespoons chopped onion or scallions
> 1 to 2 tablespoons mayonnaise

Combine all the ingredients and serve sandwich style, or scoop
onto lettuce leaves and serve as a luncheon salad.

NANCY'S BARBECUE SAUCE (1 cup) This barbecue sauce gets its bite
from fresh gingerroot. I've marinated chicken strips in it, then served
them for appetizers with extra sauce for dipping. It also works well as
a marinade or basting sauce for pork, chicken, or seafood.

> 1, 14-ounce can pineapple chunks in juice
> 1 cup prepared barbecue sauce
> 1 tablespoon fresh ginger, chopped

Drain the pineapple juice into a 2-cup container, reserving the
pineapple chunks. Add the barbecue sauce and the ginger and mix
well. Boil the leftover sauce and serve on the side with the pineapple chunks.

NANCY SHERIDAN, *Go for It*, Ericson 35

Fresh ginger adds a bite to "Nancy's Barbecue Sauce"; or gives an exotic flavor to a salad.

BREWED GINGER TEA Ginger is helpful for upset stomachs and controls nausea. When not using it to ward off queasiness, don't forget that a few pieces of slivered ginger can do wonders to zing up a marinade or add spice to a salad dressing.

To make ginger tea, simmer 1 to 1½ teaspoons fresh minced ginger in 1 cup of water for 10 minutes. Strain and sweeten with sugar if desired.

JOY OF SUMMER **GUACAMOLE** (1 cup) When sailing in the summer, I never seem to have enough hors d'oeuvres choices. I often pack an almost ripe avocado so I can whip up this zesty guacamole while the captain is uncorking the wine. If you are using a Florida avocado, double the remaining ingredients in this recipe because it is at least twice the size of its California cousin.

   1 ripe California avocado, peeled and sliced with pit removed
   Juice of half a lime (or 1 tablespoon fresh lime juice)
   1 clove garlic, minced fine or a pinch of dehydrated garlic or garlic powder
   ¼ teaspoon salt
   ¼ teaspoon dried crushed red pepper (or 1 teaspoon fresh minced jalapeño pepper)

Mash the avocado slices with a fork in a small serving bowl, then squeeze in the lime juice. Add the garlic, salt, and red pepper, and stir to blend with a fork. If you are doubling or tripling this recipe you'll find that a blender does a better job of mashing than a fork. Just toss everything in together and whirl. Serve at once with tortilla or bagel chips. Leftovers will keep a day.

Fresh limes and lemons are cherished on our boat. I also use them to garnish cocktails, flavor seafood, and wash unwanted food smells off my hands.

LIME-GRILLED SWORDFISH (2-3 servings) This recipe is low calorie and so-o-o simple. The lime rind will burn and leave the flavor cooked deliciously into the fish.

        1½ to 2 pounds swordfish
        1 fresh lime
        1 tablespoon olive oil

Rinse the swordfish and pat dry. Cut the lime into thin rounds. Baste the underside of the fish with a thin coat of olive oil. Distribute evenly the lime slices over the topside of the fish. Baste the remaining oil over the lime slices.

    Grill the underside first, for 5 to 7 minutes. With a large spatula, carefully turn the steaks by lifting and flipping them over. Keep the lime slices under the fish. Grill another 5 to 7 minutes or until the fish is cooked. Flip lime slices up onto a serving platter and enjoy.

Here are some ideas for using up eggs.

SAILBOAT DEVILED EGGS (makes 12 "boats") These little devils were created while under full sail aboard *Joy For All Seasons* homeward bound to Noank, Connecticut, from Bermuda. The sailboats floated on a fish-shaped platter and were quite delectable.

6 hard-boiled eggs	1 sheet plain white paper
3 tablespoons mayonnaise	12 toothpicks
½ teaspoon Chef Paul Prudhome's	
Magic Seasoning Blend, or to taste	

Peel the eggs, then slice in half lengthwise and slip the yolks into a small mixing bowl. Add the mayonnaise and the Seafood Magic seasoning and mash together until blended. Fill each scooped-out white with a spoonful of the yolk mixture and place on a platter. If you are doing this while under way, be sure the serving platter is secure and somewhat level.

    To complete the sailboats, cut 12 triangles from a sheet of plain white paper (white napkins or paper towels will do in a pinch). Label the sails with the names of crewmembers and their boats. For each "boat," thread a toothpick in and out of one side of the triangle, and then set one end of the toothpick into the "bow" of each egg boat.

LORRAINE MORECRAFT, *Scaramouche*[3], Tartan 41

SCRAMBLED EGGS AND ONIONS (serves 2) The onions in this egg recipe actually sweeten it, making a very pleasant combination. If you wish, add some chopped ham. For a meal under way, serve the eggs on a roll with a slice of cheese. Grill a hamburger roll, hard roll, or English muffin in the skillet just before cooking the onions.

2 tablespoons butter or margarine	**2 tablespoons milk or water**
¼ cup chopped onion	**Salt and pepper to taste**
4 eggs	

Heat the butter in a skillet over medium heat. Add the onion and sauté until it softens and begins to brown. Meanwhile, crack the eggs into a medium bowl or a large paper cup. Add the milk and scramble the mixture with a fork. Pour the egg mixture into the pan with the onions. Season with salt and pepper. Cook, mixing the eggs and onions, turning with a spatula until the eggs are done as desired. Serve with buttered toast.

"WING IT" VINAIGRETTE You don't need a recipe or a mix to make a good salad dressing. Do it the old-fashioned way by mixing the dressing right on the salad. Taste it a few times and add more of whatever is missing.

Start with a few swipes of olive oil, a few less swipes of vinegar, and season to your heart's content. If you're a novice at seasoning, sprinkle with salt and pepper to start, then add oregano, parsley, and basil. Oregano is strong, so go easy with it. Everyone will want your recipe. You can just smile smugly and tell them there *isn't* one.

Fresh fruit and vegetables on hand can be easily turned into dinner salads.

FRESH ORANGE SALAD (serves 4) Here's something simple you can do to use fresh oranges as a salad. Surprisingly easy, surprisingly good!

> **4 navel oranges, peeled and sliced in half circles**
> **2 tablespoons olive oil**
> **¼ teaspoon salt or to taste**

Combine all of the ingredients in a medium salad bowl. Chill well before serving.

TOMATO AND CUCUMBER SALAD (serves 4) This simple salad is always a hit at boat parties.

> **1 cucumber, peeled and sliced**
> **3 ripe tomatoes, sliced**
> **1 teaspoon dried oregano**
> **1 clove fresh garlic, minced fine (or a pinch of dried)**
> **3 tablespoons olive or vegetable oil**

Mix all of the ingredients together and refrigerate until ready to serve. This salad is most flavorful when made with fresh garden tomatoes. Because of the acidity in the tomatoes, you won't need to use any vinegar.

Some ideas for using fresh berries: sprinkle them on cereal; mix them into yogurt for breakfast; eat them plain as a snack; mix with other fruits and make a fruit salad; and serve them over pound cake with a dollop of whipped cream for dessert.

BLUEBERRY MUFFINS (12 muffins) These muffins are moist and delicious when hot out of the oven.

> **2 cups buttermilk baking mix**   **1 cup sour cream**
> **¼ cup sugar**   **2 tablespoons milk**
> **1 egg**   **1 cup fresh blueberries**

Preheat the oven to 400°F. In a large mixing bowl, whisk together the baking mix and sugar. In a separate bowl, beat the egg with a fork, then stir in the sour cream and milk. With a rubber spatula, fold the sour cream mixture into the dry ingredients, until just blended. Do not overmix or the biscuits will be tough. Gently stir in the berries.

To keep the blueberries from bleeding into the mix, I put them in a plastic bag along with a tablespoon of the baking mix and shake gently to coat them lightly; this seals the juices. Fill greased or paper lined muffin tins three-quarters full. Bake 10 to 12 minutes or until a toothpick inserted in the center comes out clean.

Finally, a few ideas for entrees.

BARBECUED CHICKEN STRIPS (serves 4) This is a good entrée to prepare at home and freeze, uncooked, to bring to the boat. The chicken cooks quickly on the barbecue grill, everyone likes it, and the leftovers make good snacks or sandwiches—children love them.

> 2 pounds skinless, boneless chicken breasts
> 1 cup of your favorite barbecue sauce

Rinse the chicken and pat dry, removing excess fat. Cut each breast half lengthwise into 1-inch strips, leaving the strips connected at one end for easy handling. Place the strips in a resealable plastic bag with the barbecue sauce, mix thoroughly to coat, then chill or freeze it until you are ready to cook. This is good with potato salad and some chilled baby carrots on a warm night. If there's a chill in the air, offer it with canned baked beans and buttered noodles.

LYNN FIDLER, *Fidler on the Sea*, Ericson 35

BARBECUED MEAT SANDWICHES (serves 2) This is good on a cool day when the last thing you want for lunch is a cold sandwich. I use leftover steak from the previous evening's dinner, or deli roast beef. This recipe also works with leftover pork or chicken.

> 1 cup sliced cooked steak or 6 slices deli roast beef
> ¼ cup barbecue sauce
> 2 sandwich rolls or hamburger buns

Place the barbecue sauce and beef in a skillet over medium-high heat. Sauté until the sauce bubbles and the beef is warmed. Serve on split rolls.

MAGIC SCALLOPS (serves 2-3) Grilled off the back of *Joy of Summer*, scallops prepared this way make Captain *My Way* cookie dough in my hands. He smiles and raves about the flavor so much that I wouldn't think of sailing without Paul's Magic Seasoning Blend. Any grilled fish can be prepared this way. If rain ruins your barbecue plans, sprinkle on the seasonings and sauté the scallops in a skillet down below.

> 1 tablespoon olive or vegetable oil
> 2 tablespoons dried parsley (optional)
> 1½ tablespoons Chef Paul Prudhome's Magic Seasoning Blend
> 1 pound bay scallops, rinsed and patted dry
> 3 wedges of fresh lime for garnish

Place the oil and seasonings in a resealable plastic bag with the scallops. Close the bag and mix the ingredients thoroughly to coat. Remove the scallops with a slotted spoon and place them on a hot grill on a piece of foil that's been punched with holes to allow the heat to pass through (or place on a special grill top for fish). Turn them frequently with a spatula—they'll be done in 5 minutes or less. Do not overcook or they will be tough. To serve, remove to a platter and offer with lime wedges. A packaged rice mixture makes a nice accompaniment.

It's not unusual to have someone give you fresh clams. Here is an easy way to enjoy them.

STEAMED MUSSELS OR CLAMS The hardest part of this dish is cleaning the mussels or scrubbing the clams.

> 3 to 5 pounds fresh mussels or clams in shells
> ¼ cup chopped fresh basil
> 2 tablespoons chopped fresh oregano leaves
> 1 large clove garlic, chopped
> ½ Vidalia onion, chopped
> 2 tablespoons butter
> ½ teaspoon hot sauce
> ½ fresh lemon, sliced with peel

Place the seafood in a large covered pot with 2 inches of water. Add the remaining ingredients and stir to mix. Bring to a boil. Cover the pot and reduce the heat to medium and cook until the clams or mussels open. Serve in bowls with the broth as an appetizer.

I've prepared all of these recipes in my galley, so you can, too. Don't ever be afraid to substitute or experiment—that's what makes cooking fun!

CHAPTER

13

Galley Hot Spots

ANATOMY OF A MARINE STOVE

Regardless of your boat's cooking facilities, you can almost always manage some simple cooking aboard. By their nature, marine stoves are finicky, however, and it's not uncommon for new boaters to be so intimidated by them that they hesitate to use them at first—the lighting process alone can take three steps. But if you want to use your stove for something other than as additional storage space (the oven cavity makes a great pan locker, and the stove top makes an emergency countertop), you're going to have to tackle the beast.

A marine stove is a miniature of your stove at home. It has a cooktop with two or more burners and an oven. More sophisticated stoves may even have a broiler. There are two features, though, that set it apart from your oven at home. It moves, and it has fiddles, the curved prongs that look like half smiles and that screw onto the rails of the oven top. To use fiddles, set a pan in place on a burner, then "hug" it on both sides with the clamps and tighten the screws to secure the pot in place.

Most marine stoves are gimbaled, which means that they can be latched into place to prevent them from swaying with a boat's movement, or they can be unlatched and free to swing back and forth. When alongside, most boaters latch their ovens into place. If you are cooking while under way, however, you'll want to unlatch the stove so it's free to move, thereby keeping the pans on the stove top and/or in the oven level. A gimbaled oven is especially important for offshore sailors who must cook while on passages. Unless I am cooking under way, I keep my stove in the locked position so it doesn't do the hula. Coastal sailors, like you and me, are more apt to wait until we've anchored or docked to use the stove.

No matter how good they are, marine stoves are never as efficient or reliable as their full-sized counterparts ashore. Expect oven temperatures to be erratic. Food may take longer to cook, or burn at the edges, or leave the middle uncooked. If you plan to do serious baking aboard, use an oven thermometer to monitor temperature changes.

Fumes can be dangerous, so check the stove top or oven pilot periodically to make sure it hasn't doused out mid-brownie. If your boat does not have a baking oven, and you've been craving one, investigate the possibility of an add-on. A friend of mine recently tracked down the manufacturer of her boat's ancient alcohol stove and found that she could upgrade it to include an oven. She was so thrilled with her new oven that she became a baking maniac. That summer, she kept our group provisioned with hot muffins to enjoy with our morning coffee.

The cavity of most boat ovens is small, so large pans and casserole dishes often don't fit inside. (And by the way—if you've been using your oven for storage, remember to remove these items when you light it!) Measure the oven's width, depth, and height and keep a record of the dimensions so you'll know which pan sizes will fit. I find that a 9 x 9 x 2 baking pan fits comfortably in most marine ovens. I keep one on hand for warming bread or muffins or for baking brownies or a small casserole. One-layer cake pans and six-muffin tins usually fit an oven's cavity and are perfect for baking half-batch packets of cake and muffin mixes. There's often just enough room in a marine oven to cook two frozen dinners side by side.

LIGHTING THE FIRE

Both gas- and alcohol-fueled stoves operate with pilot lights, and chances are it has been a while since you have had to ignite a pilot each time you wanted a source of cooking heat. Performing this task can be intimidating at first and, in the case of an alcohol stove, hair-raising. The new models of stoves are easier to manage than older ones because you do not need to strike a match to light them. Instead, you simply depress a button on the oven front to spark a flame (just like propane barbecue grills.)

If your stove is not equipped with an ignition button, I suggest that you keep long wooden matches or a butane igniter aboard. Matchbook matches are tidier to store but, because they have a short fuse, they will guarantee you many failed attempts and perhaps a singed fingernail or two before the fire is lit. On a gas-fueled stove, lighting a pilot is fairly simple because all you need to do is depress the oven knob, then hold it down while turning up the gas. It normally lights on the first spark and stays lit until you either turn it off or run out of fuel.

Lighting alcohol stoves, particularly the old, nonpressurized models requires patience, persistence, and courage. Each time you wish to light a burner, you must first check to be certain the alcohol reservoir is filled. Then you have to pump and pump and pump to build up pressure. Then, when you're actually ready to light the burner, you have to turn the knob—not too far, though!—and hold it in until fuel dribbles into the burner plate. And then, you strike a match. And hope. This can easily be a two-person job. Alcohol fuel lights with a burst, turns yellow, then tames to an even blue color. Once you've gotten the blue flame, you will be able to cook until the fire fizzles—and you need to repeat the procedure all over again.

We had an alcohol stove on our first boat, *Mitzi-Ann* (the Buccaneer that was named after our dog instead of me), and I clearly remember our frustration. It was a constant battle to heat anything, so I limited my cooking to heating canned soup and boiling water for instant coffee. That was also when I thought camping was fun. I learned to keep a pot of whatever I was heating already prepared and ready to pop over the licks of flame when they projected high above the burner. If I could catch that burst of heat before it died, dinner was imminent.

I also learned that it's important when lighting an alcohol stove to be fleet of foot to avoid singeing hair or other body parts, or setting the boat afire. Safety dictates that a fire extinguisher or other means of dousing an errant flame should always be handy to the galley area. Baking soda and, in the case of an alcohol fire, simple water will douse it. It all depends on the type of fuel you use.

FUEL OPTIONS

If you are thinking of buying a new boat or a new oven, it's important to understand the limitations of various types of cooking fuel. A marine gas stove will most closely resemble your stove at home, and gas is the kindest fuel to use for cooking.

Gas

Propane is the most common and most readily available cooking gas used on boats today; natural gas is the next most popular. A tank of propane gas lasts us most of the summer. Natural gas comes in smaller canisters than propane and therefore requires more frequent refilling. It also does not burn as hot, so it is less efficient than propane gas. If you find you are refilling any gas tank too often during the season, get out of that galley—you are cooking too much.

Keep in mind that all gas is explosive. You must take special precautions to prevent propane gas from leaking because it is heavier than air and will sink and may accumulate in the bilge. One flammable spark and your boating season would be over in a hurry. Gas is housed in lead containers, which are usually set within brackets in an outside locker; hosing connects the gas supply to the stove. The fuel supply can be shut off both at the tank and at an electrical panel. You or the captain should periodically check to be sure that the gas connections are snug by brushing them with soapy water. If small bubbles form, shut off the gas and tighten the connections. Read the manufacturer's manuals; it's very important to understand how to safely cook with gas aboard a boat.

Alcohol

Alcohol fuel first gained notoriety when used for campstoves. Many older boats may be equipped with alcohol stoves, so if you have bought a used boat you may be struggling with one of these horrors. Stove alcohol comes in a can and is poured directly into a receptacle in the oven itself.

Cooking on a pressurized alcohol stove is an art that is difficult to master, even on a properly working unit. Although it is possible to cook on alcohol stoves with prodding and supervision, the older style ones, especially, are often not dependable enough to be your only cooking option. If you own a stove that is fickle, be sure to have an alternate cooking plan, such as a portable grill or cooktop. Otherwise, you may one day find yourself anchored for the night with the closest restaurant a long, wet dinghy ride away.

HE SAID: *"What's for dinner?"*

SHE SAID: *"Anything you want. We're dining out!"*

I think that alcohol stoves are still an option on new boats. The new models from Sweden are nonpressurized and much more reliable than the older ones.

GO PORTABLE

Although many sleep-aboard boats are equipped with built-in cooktops and baking ovens, there are times when you'll want to use supplementary devices, such as barbecue grills and electrical appliances. If your stove or oven is inadequate or not functioning properly, portable cooking methods are even more important. There are so many options today for the traveling cook.

Propane Cooktops

Portable propane stoves have come a long way from the old-fashioned alcohol camp stoves of the past, and they have fast replaced the traditional alcohol stove in the boating world. The one-burner model operates with a canister that is easy to store and replace. Everything is contained, so no gas lines or hookups trail when you lift or move it. On a boat, a portable cooktop gives you the wherewithal to direct the captain to take that messy batch of steamers onto the dock and cook them there. Your galley will remain immaculate, cool, and fish-smell free.

I bring our portable cooktop home during the winter to use when the power goes out. It's amazing what you can prepare on only one burner. Do, however, keep spare propane canisters handy so you don't run out of gas before the food is cooked. You can find propane cooktops at camp and marine supply stores, at boat shows, and in marine catalogs.

Whenever you use a portable cooktop aboard, be certain to take the necessary precautions to prevent fire. If you are using it to replace a poorly operating stove top, perhaps you can set the portable cooktop in its well or secure it atop the original stove. If you do, be sure that your old stove is cleansed of fuel and truly non-operative. Otherwise, find a new, heatproof location to use the portable burner—perhaps in the cockpit or on a galley countertop. Ideally, any stove or grill under fire should be bolted or screwed down to a firm surface. If you have set up your cooktop in the cockpit, be sure to secure it on a fire-resistant, nonskid mat, and always keep a fire extinguisher in the galley for sudden flare-ups. This is gospel under way, but even at anchor you may get smacked silly by a passing wake. Don't take chances. You're cooking with fire.

Barbecue Grills

What's nice about barbecuing is that you can usually hand the responsibility over to the captain. However, if it rains, most likely you'll be the one who is left grumbling belowdecks pan frying the meat.

If you're new to boating and want to experiment with grilling aboard before investing in a marine barbecue, bring a small grill from home and use it on shore, or buy a one-use charcoal grill that you can discard when finished. If you find that you enjoy grilling aboard, you'll probably end up buying a kettle-style stainless steel marine grill that mounts on the transom of your boat. It is shaped like a half ball with a rounded bottom. You can even get a removable stand that will keep it erect and freestanding so you can take it ashore for beach picnics.

If your grill takes charcoal, you will likely have a partially opened bag of coal shoved away somewhere. You can't possibly imagine how messy spilt charcoal is until the first time you open a locker and find everything in it covered with black ick. I speak from experience. Water seeped into our lazarette, where we stowed our charcoal, and the black soot became black syrup, oozing everywhere. Save yourself the aggravation of cleaning up such a mess by investing in a zippered, waterproof charcoal bag; they even have a pocket to hold lighter fluid.

There are so many cooking choices to consider when you

begin boating, but it always comes down to compactness and functionality. Think before you buy. What will you grill? Hamburgers? Fish? Roasts? Will the size of the grill accommodate the quantity you will need to cook for your family, as well as a few guests? The size, shape, and fuel source of the grill that best meets your needs will become clearer as your first boating season progresses. Take it slow. Start cheap and small, then decide if and when you need to upgrade.

Try the Electric Slide

This idea may not appeal to you if you are a true camper trying to get away from it all, but electricity can be one solution to portable cooking as long as you have access to dockside power. Take to the boat your electrical cooking appliances—an electric fry pan, a drip coffeepot, a toaster, even a tiny microwave. They will all make your life easier, although they will be a nuisance to stow and won't work once you pull away from the dock. Learn to use your boat's cooking facilities so when you are nestled in a pretty harbor you won't be trying to coax a flame out of a stove you may have never used. Always have an alternate meal plan. Check out your waterway guide, talk to your friends, and do whatever it takes to get information about restaurants at your destination.

CHAPTER

14

Cold Places

USING AN ICE CHEST

Keeping food and drinks cold on a boat can be as difficult as winning the America's Cup Race. Your boat may be equipped with anything from a portable cooler to a full-sized refrigerator—although if you have a full-sized refrigerator you are probably on a huge powerboat or living in a house.

There are typically two methods for keeping food cold on most boats—in an ice chest, or box, where the sole source of coolant is ice; or in a refrigerator that consists of an ice chest that is equipped with coils, through which a coolant is circulated (in a manner similar to a household refrigerator). Regardless of how it's kept cool, a marine ice chest is usually top loading and deep, requiring one to dive in head first to retrieve something from its floor—not

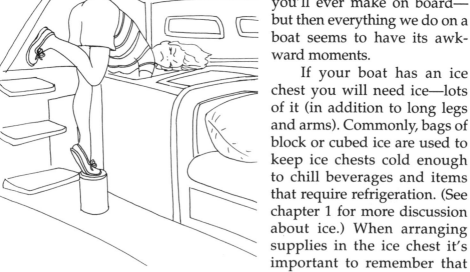

exactly the most graceful move you'll ever make on board—but then everything we do on a boat seems to have its awkward moments.

If your boat has an ice chest you will need ice—lots of it (in addition to long legs and arms). Commonly, bags of block or cubed ice are used to keep ice chests cold enough to chill beverages and items that require refrigeration. (See chapter 1 for more discussion about ice.) When arranging supplies in the ice chest it's important to remember that heat rises. Therefore, store the ice as high up in the chest as you can—on a shelf if the chest is equipped with one. The size and shape of the chest and the quality of its insulation are the key determinants of how long ice will last on your boat.

For example, the ice chest on our previous boat, *Joy of Summer*, was about 12 cubic feet. For a weekend trip we started with one block of ice and two bags of cubes. On stays lasting more than a weekend, we started with two blocks of ice and two bags of cubes. We added one bag of cubes each day we were aboard; on longer trips, we added a new block every few days.

It won't take long before you can estimate how long a block or bag will keep in your ice chest. Blocks generally remain solid about four times longer than the same weight in cubes because of their density, so be sure to include at least one block of ice in your start-up supply.

Averting the Avalanche Effect

One of the hardest parts of dealing with an ice chest is that it suffers from the avalanche effect. This is how it goes. One of the kids reaches into the chest for a soda and, kerplunk! Everything that formerly rested atop that soda is now vying for the empty spot below. Stalks of celery shift out of their packaging and sit indignantly in the water at the base of the cooler, socializing with the container of milk and the carton of eggs that is now half-opened and upside down. When you open the chest to make lunch, the baloney is swimming.

Here's how I suggest keeping this problem somewhat under control:

○ Nag, nag, nag until your crew becomes more careful.
○ Off-load popular beverages from the ice chest and put them into a separate cooler to limit access to your domain.
○ Guard the ice chest lid with your life. The more frequently it is opened, the sooner food will spoil and the messier it will become.
○ Organize supplies in the ice chest so you can quickly locate them.
○ Package loose foods together and out of the way.

After years of fiddling with ways to pile food into this cavern, I learned to arrange items so they are protected and even mildly accessible. Here's how: Put heavy items, such as large cans, bottles, and cartons of soda, milk, and juice, upright in the bottom of the ice chest and lightweight and crushable ones on top. Try to place supplies in the same general spot each time you stay aboard so you can easily locate them. Plastic can dispensers are convenient for keeping cans of soda and beer organized and together. Place the bags of ice on top of the beverages and well-wrapped meat and seafood. As the ice melts it will leave an inch or two of water at the base of the chest, which will contribute toward keeping the chest cold. (It does the same in portable coolers.) However, you will want to get rid of the excess water so the provisions won't drown. Most chests have a very small drain for the water to exit, but they are notorious for getting clogged with bits of paper and debris; others incorporate a pump to get rid of the water. Leave about one inch of water in the chest for cooling. Be careful to keep paper packaging and unsealed foods away from the bottom of the chest to avoid a soggy mess. As I wrote earlier, place dinner meats and seafood, tightly and protectively wrapped, directly under an ice block or bag in the coldest part of the ice chest.

To organize small items, I place them in supermarket plastic bags with handles. Covered plastic containers work well also, but they require more structured space. Group and protect cheeses, dips, vegetables, fruits, and breads and other lightweight packaged goods by sorting them into two or three different bags or containers. Keep one bag for yogurt, cheese, butter, and packaged dips; another for lettuce, celery, and carrots; and a third for deli meats, sausage sticks, and other snack foods. It may even be possible to screw cup hooks on the sides of the ice chest to hang bags up and out of the way.

When you need to retrieve something from the bottom of the chest, just grab the handles of the plastic bags or pick up the plastic containers and take them out—but don't forget to replace them when you are through. Between several bags of ice, beverages, and foods, ice chests tend to get crowded and overloaded. If this is a problem on your boat, simply remove the beverages and ice them down in a separate cooler. If you're sailing in cold waters, you can even chill nonperishable drinks by dangling them overboard in a retrievable net.

Cleaning an Ice Chest

As the ice melts in a chest, it will eventually soak off paper labels and saturate cardboard milk and juice cartons. You will need to keep a close watch on small items because they will sink lower by the hour and tumble into the pool of water at the bottom of the chest. This is why it's important to frequently clean and reorganize an ice chest.

I like to tackle this job just after breakfast or before I grocery shop because it gives me a chance to see what I have and to toss out anything foul. You'll find that this isn't the monster of a project you'd thought. In five or ten minutes you can sort through the contents, wipe up spills, pump out extra water, and discard past-their-prime foods. Restock beverages and add fresh ice if you need it. If your chest has an interior shelf, tuck a box of baking soda on it to keep the chest smelling fresh; if there is no dry place to put it, use a refrigerator deodorizer that's encased in plastic.

It is especially important to attend to the ice chest before leaving to go home. The first time you forget will usually be the last because, upon your return, a putrid odor—a combination of spoiled food and mildew—will assault you when you lift the lid. The black gook you'll see is mold. So before you leave, empty the chest entirely and pump out all the water. Metal cans will leave rusty rings if left at the bottom of the ice chest for long periods of time, and paper labels on bottles will certainly disintegrate. Most items will be wet when you take them out. If they are unopened and can survive without refrigeration, set them on paper towels in the sink or on the countertop where they will drain and dry while you are away.

Wipe down the interior of the chest, using the cleanser of your choice. Baking soda and water freshens and sweetens the chest, and Lysol disinfectant prevents, but does not kill, mildew. I use both, as the mood strikes me. If I notice some mildew forming, I use a mild solution of chlorine and water to kill the spores. I premix and store this solution in an old spray bottle so it's always readily available. Leave the ice chest lid open while you are away to allow the interior to dry completely. Pack perishable items into a cooler, along with some leftover ice, for the trip home.

REFRIGERATION

What a luxury onboard refrigeration is. Our new boat is equipped with it, and now I wonder how we ever existed without it—one more step into the civilized world. But with refrigeration comes complexity. We stop simply trooping off to the nearest shoreside supply to get bags of cubes or blocks, and turn to a more complex world of mechanical and electrical gear.

Some marine refrigerators are driven directly by the boat's engine; others are powered by the boat's batteries, which, in turn, need to be amply charged by the engine or a generator. Still another source of needed power can be provided by 110-AC volt shore power.

If you are in a slip, you can simply plug in to shore power and reap the joys of refrigeration. You will be able to leave the refrigerator on when you go home. When you return to the boat, it will be to perfectly chilled beverages and firm sticks of butter. Refrigerators keep a consistent temperature, so your packing and shuttling loads will be lighter because you can use your boat refrigerator like the one at home. The only ice you'll need is for drinks, and you will require less because it will stay solid much longer. But the best part is that your food will no longer be waterlogged, and all that space you used for storing multiple blocks and bags of ice is freed. We always keep a bag or two of ice in our refrigerator for drinks (and it helps maintain the cold in the ice chest throughout the heat of the day).

If you are on a mooring or frequently at anchor, you may find that refrigeration is less of a boon because it is more of a challenge to maintain consistent temperature. Unless you have an inverter and/or a generator to provide additional power to maintain the operation of a refrigerator without draining your batteries, you will use it sporadically and do most of your chilling with ice.

We learned how to operate a boat with refrigeration when chartering in the islands where ice is scarce and on-board refrigeration is a necessity. To charge the refrigerator and maintain cold temperatures, you must run the engine for a few hours each day, once in the morning and again at night. The temperature should then hold in between the two charging periods. It's nice to do as much of the charging as you can when you're naturally under power—while raising the anchor, entering and exiting harbors and marinas, and the like. Inevitably, though, you'll have to run the engine or generator while sitting at anchor or on a mooring. It is noisy, so if you are in a marina be considerate of your neighbors.

We usually keep our refrigeration set at about 40°F so food won't freeze. Monitor the temperature gauge when you are charging the refrigeration to determine how long it takes to reach your goal. Once you do this, you will know how long you need to run the engine or generator to maintain fresh food. Naturally, continually turning the refrigeration on and off will mean that the temperature won't be as consistent as it would be if it were plugged into shore power. Also, you must still clean out the refrigerator when you leave for home, unless you have a means to keep it charged while you are away.

PART FOUR

Nautical Exposures

YOU'RE OUT THERE, unprotected, prey to the elements, the ailments, and anything else that comes along. Understanding how to cope with nature is your gateway to conquering "outer space." So many natural fabrics, new sun care products, natural medicines, and other helpful items work to protect you from whatever discomforting evils may befall you while boating. Use the products of your choice and beat the odds.

CHAPTER

15

Sun, Wind, and Chilly Weather

KEEPING BODY AND SOUL TOGETHER

The sun beating down on you, the rain pounding on your head, the wind dancing through your hair, and the humidity ruining your hairdo—this is boating at its finest. By the time you realize you won't melt from the heat and you don't really care about your hairdo or makeup anyhow, it's probably too late. Your skin is dry and peeling, gaining momentum toward early wrinkledom, and your hair feels like a straw broom. Mend your errant ways and take positive action.

AVOIDING LIZARD SKIN, OR WORSE

A fake tan won't cost you as much as a real one. Pick your flavor from honey to bronze and you'll avoid the onset of crinkly leathery skin commonly found on lizards. You may easily fool yourself into thinking that the wonderful warm sun and a refreshing breeze are healthy, and they are—in sensible doses. As a boater, however, you're overexposed to all the elements and a prime candidate for skin cancer, sun poisoning, windburn, and sunburn. Look around you. Everything is reflective—from the shiny hull of your boat to the water you're sailing in. The wind and sails may tease you into feeling cool and shaded, but the hazards of exposure are there.

Take the same precautions when sailing that you would if you were sunbathing on a beach. Your skin needs moisture as well as good sun protection. Don't bother with any sun lotion under 15 SPF and make sure it's waterproof, or at least sweat proof, and remember that you can get burned on even the foggiest day. Several fine sun care lines have been developed specifically for mariners. Opt for makeup and lip balms with sunscreen, and keep aloe on board to soothe sunburn. Even if you've been smart, most captains think they are invincible, and most guests will want to work on their tans.

SHE SAID: *"Put on some lotion."*
HE SAID: *"I don't need any. I'm wearing a hat."*
(Later)
HE SAID: *"Do we have any aloe on board?"*

Children have delicate skin and risk severe sunburn. Further, they are constantly running in and out of the water, rinsing off any sun protection that you or their moms might've gotten them to hold still for. Swathe them with a waterproof, high SPF sunblock. There are many products made just for children that also work well for adults with sensitive skin, or for the face. Make certain that adults and children alike drink plenty of fluids to avoid dehydration, which can result in sunstroke.

Sun poisoning may appear as itchy bumps in overexposed areas or as edema. When I have been in the sun too long, I often get rashes on my chest and arms; when my husband makes the same mistake, his ankles swell. If you are sailing and can't take a break from the sun, cover your sun-tired areas and look for shade. I find a mild antihistamine taken according to package directions reduces itching and swelling, so I always keep a bottle of it in my travel case. Learn the danger signs of skin cancer and schedule periodic skin checks. Having fun in the sun is like playing with fire; it can blow up on you if you don't pay attention. Take appropriate precautions, and no one will be able to tell by looking at your skin that you are a boater.

HEAD CARE

Always wear a visor or hat to protect your skin and hair from sun and windburn. Clip-on visors are comfortable, chic, won't ruin your hairdo or fly off your head under way, and are available in an assortment of flattering colors and styles. Keep in mind, however, that a visor will only shade your face and eyes. Men usually prefer baseball caps, but unless they're worn backward they won't protect them from crocodile neck.

A full coverage, brim style sun hat offers the most protection, especially if constructed of a sunblock fabric. The bigger the brim, though, the more likely it is that a hat will take flight on a windy sail. So, choose a style with a chinstrap or a clip to secure it to your clothes. I have to admit that I bought a brimmed hat equipped with a chinstrap on the recommendation of my dermatologist. It looked fetching on the salesperson at the boat show booth, but dorky on me. I only wear it under duress or when my captain and I are sailing alone. I did, however, recently wear it on a seven day offshore passage (I wanted to hide my hair and the trip qualified as duress). When I arrived home, I was delighted to find that my hair didn't get dry as straw and, because my face had been shaded, I had fewer freckles and less tan than I would've gotten on a sailing vacation. There *are* benefits to not caring how we look.

Many women boaters brag that we don't give a hoot about our hair, but I think that's only a way of justifying that devil-may-care coiffure we sport most of the summer. Hair that's blowing in the wind might look sexy in advertisements, but you'll observe that ads never show how tangled and matted the hair is when the wind stops blowing.

Between the wind and the sun, your hair hasn't got a chance unless you take some measures to protect it. A visor keeps short hair off the face. For longer hair, cover it with a hat, stuff it in a cap, or gather it into a ponytail or braid before you set out. Restyling will be a cinch compared with undoing wind tangles, and your sail will be more enjoyable without your hair slapping against your face. You can also load up your locks with hair conditioner and slick them back for a day in the sun. If you use enough, people will think your hair's just wet from a swim.

If you've gone ahead and done the deed and you're stuck dealing with abused hair, the comb out will be less excruciating if you first spritz on some conditioner before using a wide-toothed comb to untangle the mess. This works especially well for long hair, which can be mercilessly matted by the end of a boating trip.

If you have been out for a long sail, gotten doused with sea spray, or have gone swimming, it's important to get rid of the salt residue from your hair as soon as possible. Salt can damage colored, highlighted, or permed hair because it may chemically react. Regardless, salt air settles like a veil on hair, leaving it sticky, a bit stiff, and crusty. If you can't shampoo right away, rinsing your hair with plain water will work, too; in a pinch, a bottle of club soda will do. If you swim daily, use a shampoo that's designed to remove chemical buildup, and don't forget to slather on conditioner. Look for shampoos with sun protection; brands that double as a body wash (a space-saving convenience); and soaps that lather in salt water. Whatever kind you use, your final rinse should always be with fresh water. Every little bit of effort you make will help a dry, lifeless mop feel like real hair again.

COVER-UP

Know when you've had enough. You'll be spending long days exposed to the elements, so take your time—you don't need to get a tan in one day. Always use a sunblock with a minimum SPF of 15 or above (more is better), then cover up or get out of the glare. If you have fair skin that burns easily, a long-sleeved shirt, lightweight long pants, and socks may become your standard sunny day attire. Hands and forearms take a beating on a boat. Coat them with sunblock and wear your sailing gloves while under way. On a blazing hot day, swim in a T-shirt to avoid burning your back. Having a sunburn and not being able to get out of the sun can be mighty uncomfortable on a long day sail, particularly if all you have aboard are shorts and swimsuits. Always bring along cover-up clothes and extra hats. If you have sun-sensitive skin, entire clothing lines—shirts, pants, and hats—have been designed to act as a 30+ SPF sunscreen.

WATCH THOSE PEEPERS

You've only got one set of eyes and they have to last you your lifetime. Don't squint. Invest in polarized sunglasses to protect your eyes from damaging ultraviolet rays. White circles around your eyes can be blended to match the rest of your tanned face with a dab of makeup, but crinkles last forever. Mariners' sunglasses take a beating—when salt water dries it forms crystals that are notorious for eroding mirror coatings on lenses—so it's a good practice to clean your glasses after each day on the water to remove sea spray and sun oils.

My sunglasses are prescription lenses, so I keep an old pair aboard to use strictly for sailing. At a recent boat show, we discovered stick-on plastic magnifying spots that convert regular sunglasses to bifocals for reading. The "spots" are available in different magnification levels and can be removed, then re-adhered. My captain bought a set and can now read charts when we're under way without having to deal with a separate pair of glasses swinging on his chest, or he can read a book on the beach without wearing two sets of glasses and looking ridiculous.

A spare pair of inexpensive regular sunglasses is convenient to have aboard to loan guests who forgot theirs or say they never wear them, or to replace glasses that have fallen in the drink. Keep all eyewear intact with eyeglass holders, those string devices that attach to glasses, and keep them securely around your neck when you are not wearing them. It's quite disconcerting to have to send a diver down to retrieve glasses you absolutely need in order to see. Most eyeglass holders are inexpensive enough so you can afford an assortment to coordinate with your outfits. I found a thin leather holder that is particularly comfortable to wear because it doesn't catch in my hair or stick onto my neck or collar. Eyeglass holders are also helpful if you need to switch often from sunglasses to clear glasses. You can just wear the second pair dangling on your chest and pull up whichever you need at the time.

DRINK UP

If you start to feel a bit listless, or can't remember the last time you've been to the head, have a soft drink or a cup of water. One of the more common afflictions on the water is dehydration. The sun and wind sap fluids out of our systems without us realizing it, as do many of the salty snacks we continually munch on. Keep a tall, cool, glass of water or other nonalcoholic beverage by your side to sip on throughout the day. Water is the best for staying hydrated, but any nonalcoholic or decaffeinated liquid will do. Allot at least a quart of water or other liquid per person per day.

Keep an eye on guests when under way. Offer them soft
drinks frequently and remember that some folks will avoid drinking fluids so they won't have to deal with using the head on your
boat. Sometimes they have a good reason. We had one friend who
was horrified when the holding tank split after she used our
head, spewing green ooze all over the cabin sole. We had to hose
that mess down and dispense of it through the bilge. Of course, it
wasn't her fault. The holding tank was defective. But I have yet to
convince her otherwise.

Beware the Devil Rum

Beware of boaters' cocktail hour. The social drinking that goes on
amongst sailors can creep up on the least suspecting, and soon we
are swilling regularly and gaining weight. (Where do you think
the terms "drunken sailor" and "rummy" come from?) Mild consumption of alcoholic beverages that normally would be okay
may contribute to problems on the water. A day in the wind and
blazing sun—which makes some people dizzy—is dehydrating,
and so is alcohol. Double trouble. To put drinking into perspec-
tive, most weekend sailors are not alcoholics, but those of us who
literally *live* on our boats all summer and enjoy cocktails each
evening sometimes have a problem getting back to normal once
boat season ends.

I can't always keep up with the cocktail crowd at our marina.
I abhor waking up at three o'clock in the morning with a pounding
headache and a wild thirst for water, and feeling miserable a good
part of the following day. Summer's too short! Alcohol also con-
flicts with many medications and makes hot flashes more intense.
So, if you're a nondrinker, or a light drinker like me, treat yourself
to a "perception" cocktail. Pour ginger ale or seltzer into a cham-
pagne glass, or fill a wine glass with lemonade, then join the gang
in the cockpit to watch the sunset. Just holding a stemmed glass
will make you feel festive.

For virgin drinks, add lots of mixer and ice in your favorite
glass. I make semi-virgins by tossing a splash of liquor on top of a
full glass of iced tonic water or my favorite mixer. The mix gives
me a satisfying first sip that fools me into thinking the entire drink
will taste the same. And, I almost always garnish with a lemon,

lime, cherries, olives, or a slice of fresh peach. The psychological impact is amazing. Remember that most blender drinks are fattening though, even without the booze.

FOUL-WEATHER GEAR

There's no alternative. You will need a set of good foul-weather gear. The shortest sail will feel like an ocean crossing when you're soaked to the skin and shivering. The old-fashioned rubber stuff you may remember is obsolete. Today's new fabrics and construction methods keep you bone dry while allowing air to circulate. Buy the whole deal—the jacket, pants, and boots.

The sou'wester hat that's advertised in all the boating magazines is darling, and I couldn't resist buying one, but I've only worn it once. I looked like a yellow duck once I added it to the rest of my foul-weather attire. I gave it to a friend who had always wanted one. Maybe a sou'wester will be more flattering on you. It will prevent rain from running inside your collar, but that's not an essential quality unless your rain jacket doesn't have a hood.

Rubber sea boots have a multitude of uses. They slip nicely over a pair of warm socks, keep your feet dry and warm, and give you the deck traction you'll need during downpours under way. You can also wear them ashore in the rain (you'll look either nautical or goofy), to bail out the dinghy, or to dig for clams. During the winter, slip them over thick socks when you're shoveling snow from your driveway or mopping water out of your basement.

When you buy foul-weather gear, pick a color that will show up against the ocean. If you should be tossed overboard while wearing it, your chances of being rescued are reduced if the color of your clothes blends into the water. Raucous yellow and bright orange are the most easily seen colors, especially in fog, rain, and at night. The set of yellow gear I recently purchased has an atrocious chartreuse hood that, happily, entirely folds in under the collar. When I asked the salesperson why it was such a horrible color, I was told it was for prominence in the water. The color red is a good second choice, but blue, white, and green gear is invisible in the water.

Sometimes, you won't want to bother donning the entire foul-weather uniform—you'll probably wear the jacket more than any other piece—but do keep all of it aboard so it will be there when you need it. While anchored near Newport, Rhode Island, one horrendously rainy Saturday, a group of us abandoned our ships to go ashore. It was raining so hard that we had to wear full gear—pants, jackets, boots, and hats—just to get from our boats into our car without getting drenched. We drove into Newport to shop and have lunch, figuring we would peel down to our street clothes when we arrived. No such luck! It was raining just as hard there. We didn't take our gear off until many hours later when we were safely back inside our boats.

A full set of high-quality foul-weather gear can easily cost well over $200. It pays to investigate all of the major brands. Each makes many different styles of gear, ranging from lightweight, simple models for weekend coastal sailors, to heavyweight, extremely complex models for serious offshore sailors. Keep an open mind and consult your pocketbook. Evaluate how often you intend to use it and how comfortable you want to be. You can get started with an inexpensive set of rainwear that comes packed in a plastic bag for less than $10. I keep several sets of these in a variety of sizes aboard for guests. They don't look very fashionable, but they're popular items on a stormy day.

HE SAID: *"Where's my jacket?"*

SHE SAID: *"You wore it home last weekend."*

When your gear gets wet, hang it in an open area to dry completely before stowing so it won't get mildewed. Some boaters sprinkle baby powder on their foul-weather clothes to absorb extra moisture before putting them away—that's especially important if you keep your suit folded. Should you happen to wear your foul-weather gear home, don't forget to bring it back to the boat. You never know when you're going to need it.

WARM STUFF

Nylon or synthetic windbreakers and wind suits, as well as anything made of polar fleece, offer good protection against dampness and cool, windy conditions. Before you hit the malls and marine stores, experiment with items in your coat closet to find out if what you have already will work for you. When you are ready to supplement your existing gear, buy carefully with an eye for weatherability. Remember that you can always put a foul-weather jacket over whatever you're wearing.

Ten percent of our body heat is lost through our head, hands, and feet. Hats, hoods, ski masks, full-fingered sailing gloves, and heavy socks give added warmth and comfort while sailing. I always keep spare sweatshirts, jackets, and sweatpants aboard. I get cold easily and there are days when I'm not too proud to wear three jackets, a pull-on cap and hood over my head, and double mittens to keep warm. Don't overlook ski masks if you're into frigid-weather sailing. There are also polar fleece head and face coverings that can be worn scrunched down like a turtleneck.

A set of long underwear is basic gear for cool weather boating, and you can also sleep in it. Silk is my favorite fabric because it's lightweight, warm, and takes little storage space, but it sometimes isn't sufficiently toasty on a very cool, gusty day. Sport stores and catalogs offer many choices appropriate to various temperatures and conditions. Make sure that the long underwear is made of fabric that wicks, or draws moisture away from your skin. Wool is a natural wicking fiber, which is why it traditionally has been a popular, although sometimes itchy, cold weather choice. Cotton is not. It is absorptive, so when worn as an underlayer it will trap body sweat and may make you feel cold and clammy in cool weather. Many new synthetic blends are superior to most natural fibers because they are comfortable, nonabsorptive, and keep you feeling warm and dry.

EXTRA PROTECTION

Most boats come with a minimum of overhead protection. Powerboats have hard windshields that allow crew to dodge sea spray at high speeds and their cockpits can easily be enclosed with vinyl and canvas. Powerboats also skim atop the water and do not depend on wind to keep them going, so adding height is not the detriment to boat speed it is in a sailboat. The nature of a sailboat is to offer as little resistance to the wind as possible to gain speed and mobility. A purist sailor relies strictly on the shade of flying sails for wind and sun protection because boats with low profiles (no dodgers, no biminis) have less resistance and can move more quickly.

Cower Under a Dodger

People never think they really need a luxury item until they've enjoyed its convenience on someone else's boat. If you're on a boat budget, and most of us are, the workhorse of frills is the dodger. A dodger does just what its name implies. It deflects sea spray coming over the bow and provides some protection from the wind and sun.

On a powerboat, a dodger often takes the form of a hard windshield with a canvas or fiberglass hood. On a sailboat, the windshield is clear vinyl and inset into a canvas cap. It snaps on just forward of the companionway and is usually tall enough and extends far enough into the cockpit to cover the companionway opening. The dodger umbrellas the companionway, repelling rain while allowing cool air in. It will keep some degree of rain and water out from belowdecks and provide enough protective seating for two people, one on each side. Cower under it while the helmsman plays master of the ship and you can avoid the sun, the wind, the rain, and the cold in its lee.

When ordering a canvas dodger for a sailboat, make sure its design provides enough room to duck comfortably beneath it to go belowdecks. We've got battle scars on our foreheads and backs from our first dodger. Chrome piping forms the support structure for a canvas dodger. Test yours to be certain it is sturdy enough to support a person's weight because people tend to grab onto it when boarding the boat or going forward. On a sunny, sultry day, you can unzip the vinyl windows for ventilation but remain shaded. For extra seating space when you're hosting a crowd, or when racing, you can fold the dodger back or remove it.

Bask under a Bimini

I had to go to the Caribbean to really discover the benefits of a bimini top, a semi-permanent canvas top that keeps the sun and rain out of the cockpit. Think of a canvas bimini as an extension of a dodger. If you plan it right, one zips on to the other. Powerboaters thought of the concept of a bimini top long before sailors.

Many larger powerboats have pilothouses, which allow the helmsmen to operate their boats "indoors." Some sailboats—particularly those designed for heavy weather and year-round sailing—also have pilothouses. The ones that I've toured at boat shows seem to have less headroom below; the pilothouse digs into precious living space. The more common solution for warm-weather pleasure sailors looking for shade, ventilation, and optimum living space is a bimini.

A canvas bimini will extend the coverage of your dodger to include the overhead area of the cockpit, thereby keeping even the helmsman drier than usual and protected against the sun. And, unless you are experiencing heavy weather or trying to make speed in a race, you can sail with a bimini up, so order one with a window so you can view the mainsail. A bimini folds out of the way when you want to enjoy the sun and is easily erected when you've had enough. It keeps your cockpit dry overnight, so anyone sleeping there won't wake up wet with morning dew.

Of course, one thing leads to another. Now you're ready to think about zip-on plastic side and aft panels so you can convert your cockpit into a soft pilothouse. While you are shopping for all this, you'll probably convince yourself that you need a set of those matching hatch and winch covers, too.

Stay Cool under a Suncover

Suncovers are most prevalent on sailboats because their cockpits are exposed to the weather. The sun beating down on a boat can be merciless in creating ovenlike temperatures belowdecks. Suncovers may be custom ordered or homemade. If you are buying or making one, treated canvas is the best fabric choice. In a pinch you can always flop a flat white bed sheet over the boom and tie the corners to the railings, halyards, or whatever is handy to get a similar effect. Designed to be used while your boat is anchored, moored, or docked, a suncover ties on with a series of lines and covers the area from the mainsail, aft. Be sure to remove it and fold it away before you set sail because it will be in the way.

16

Protection Under Way

MOTION MADNESS

There you are sitting in your cockpit enjoying a wonderful sail. The sails are set and need little tending, so you decide to refresh beverages and bring up the makings for tuna fish sandwiches for lunch. Suddenly, your boat feels like it's gotten whacked by a whale. You pitch first to one side, then to the other. The sails bang and flap in vehement protest. The cockpit becomes a milkshake. The bag of potato chips, cans of coke, and the bowl of tuna salad slide from side to side until the wake from the powerboat has finished rippling toward you.

The captain shakes his fist at the boat and shouts obscenities, but it's too late—the offending boat is long gone. You feel wet and icky and realize that the tuna bowl is upside down in your lap and soda is draining all over the cockpit. You make a vow to prepare sandwiches in advance next time and install a drink holder for the soda cans. A bruise is brewing on your left knee and one of the kids is crying. There's a yelp from below and you remember that someone was using the head; he emerges a ghastly shade of green. (During one other such lurch, a visiting friend using the head hit the door with such impact that she went flying out into the saloon, toilet seat and all. Fortunately, she was more surprised and embarrassed than hurt.)

You will experience a wide range of motion on a sailboat, from the gentle, cradlelike rock at anchor, to the sudden jolt from the nasty wake of a powerboat, to the exaggerated movement under way caused by 25-knot winds or 8-foot seas. No matter which style of boat you own—powerboat, sailboat, or trawler—at any given time you are apt to encounter erratic movement, resulting in getting hit by flying objects, nausea, motion fatigue, or minor injuries. Eventually, though, as you become more comfortable aboard under way, you'll learn to anticipate these conditions and prepare yourself to keep side effects at bay.

SOMEBODY'S SICK

If you are someone who gets sick looking at a glass of water, boating may present a problem for you. But don't give up the ship until you've talked with your doctor about medications that might help you keep the effects of undulation under control. We all suffer occasional bouts of nausea. The symptoms vary from listlessness to vomiting, but they all add up to the same thing. A seasick person needs help. Be sensitive to the likelihood of seasickness of those sailing with you. Men, especially, hate to admit to it.

Always ask guests if they are on medication for seasickness, so you won't be alarmed if they fall asleep at the helm, and don't offer alcoholic beverages until you're sure their medication has worn off. Some medications are effective for as long as 24 hours. If a person is quiet or looks pale, urge him or her to sip some ginger ale, insist they wear acupressure bands, and position him or her facing the wind. Those who suspect that they will have a problem with seasickness should take preventative measures. The new, improved version of the Transderm patch has recently returned to the market and is available by prescription. I am told that many of the negative side effects of the original patch have been remedied. The patch is an especially good solution for people who are chronically seasick and expect to be on the water for more than a few hours. For the occasional bout of mal de mer, however, most of us use an over-the-counter medication. Naturally, it's important to read and follow the directions for each. To work properly, most medications need to be taken one hour or more prior to departure. Some medications are antidrowsy. If yours isn't, perhaps a half dose will be sufficient to stave off queasiness, yet keep you alert for the sail.

Ginger is a natural seasickness remedy. You can purchase ginger capsules at a health food store, or keep ginger ale, ginger cookies, or candied ginger aboard. Even ground ginger will work—you only need to take about one quarter of a teaspoonful to do the job. I also keep several pairs of acupressure wristbands aboard. They alleviate or prevent nausea using pressure-point therapy, and it's

never too late to slip on a pair. The bands are one of the few reme-
dies that can help once a person is stricken. You can purchase them
almost anywhere for about $10.

Other than these items, standard motion sickness equipment is
a bucket, a damp towel, and some common sense. Every sailor has
made the mistake of vomiting overboard into the wind. We only
make it once. If a crewmember complains of nausea or dizziness,
position him or her on the side of the boat away from the wind—
the "lee." Being sick over the lee side makes a lousy experience a
bit less traumatic and messy for everyone.

If seasickness has reached the projectile level, tend to sick people with compassion. Offer room-temperature liquids and plain
crackers. A little food in their stomachs may help stabilize the condition. Give them a cool wet cloth to wipe their face and help them
feel refreshed. This is not a good time to tell war stories about your
bouts with nausea, or to make descriptive comments about food.
Once the worst is past, see if you can get them to take the helm for
a bit. Looking at a fixed point on the horizon, coupled with the
challenge of steering the vessel, may distract them from their
symptoms.

A boat is always moving, even when at a dock, and there is
no such thing as a person who never gets sick. The right (or
wrong) combination of conditions can affect anyone. Each person
handles motion stress differently. For example, very slow rocking
and following seas are two conditions that get my stomach churn-
ing. The important thing is to understand which actions cause
problems for you and your crew so you know when to take precautions. After you've been boating a while, you'll instinctively
know what *not* to do.

Preventing Seasickness

In the old days, sailors used to indulge in a heavy meal before setting out in order to ward off seasickness. Eat, drink, and be merry,
but *do* use common sense. Remember how you felt that time you
ate a sausage grinder and then rode the roller coaster at an amuse-
ment park? Sometimes it's not how much you eat, but how di-
gestible it is. While it's important to keep tummies full and thirst
quenched, my experience is that rich, spicy foods and heavy sailing

don't mix. Save pepperoni sticks, garlicky dips, and chocolates for when you're nearing your destination and you won't have to live with them, or see them again.

One stormy weekend not too long ago, my captain brought our boat down to Connecticut from Rhode Island at the beginning of the boating season with a few of his male chums. They began the day with huge breakfasts of sausages and triple-egg omelets and lord knows what else. It turned out to be a rough ride home—30-knot winds and large swells washing over the bow into the cockpit. All of them, even my captain who should have known better, were ill. We had a similar experience when chartering in Tahiti. Our cook prepared us a breakfast of French toast fried in bacon grease before our journey. We saw our breakfast all the way to Bora Bora.

There is a better chance of keeping seasickness under control if you encourage people to remain in the cockpit where there's plenty of fresh air. Although it's normal to close portholes and hatches to keep water out of the boat while under way, doing so means that ventilation is poor belowdecks. Using the head can be a particularly harrowing experience that can tip the scales for anyone on the verge of illness, yet sometimes that's where he or she needs to be. By its nature, the head is a confined area, and people feel bound to close the door, even if there's no one else around.

Spending time below while under way can bring on or aggravate nausea because of the rolling and heeling of the boat. I have always envied those who have such a strong constitution that they can go below and read, do crosstitch, and perform a multitude of other tasks that I must put off doing until we dock.

SOMEBODY'S INJURED

Common sense, a think-before-you-move attitude, and a pair of comfortable sailing gloves and deck shoes are a head start to preventing injuries while the boat is in motion. The wind is a power you learn to respect, especially if you have a sailboat. It creates a tremendous force on the lines and, unless you are in control, you can suffer serious rope burns, pinched fingers, and a multitude of other catastrophes. Accidents can happen very quickly under way, particularly in heavy or gusty winds, so it's important to keep your body parts away from loose, flapping lines that can smack you in the face, wrap around your legs, or trip you overboard.

SAILING GLOVES

Sailing gloves are a critical tool of our sport. Get yourself a sturdy pair—leather ones last longest. Put them on before you set sail and keep them on because, as soon as you remove them, the captain will ask you to haul up the mainsail. If you often have guests aboard, especially strong men who can't wait to winch in a sail, keep a spare pair aboard for them. They'll want to come back more often if they don't go home with inflamed palms. Sailing gloves also do a good job of preventing calluses and rope burns.

Like most women sailors, I wear gloves to keep my hands soft and feminine. Our hands and forearms are exposed areas that receive a lot of sun, leaving us with unattractive freckles and leathery skin. My sailing gloves double as extra sunscreen for the backs of my hands. Gloves with cut-off fingers spell disaster for manicures and, although long nails and sailing don't mix, you can still keep pretty nails if you wear full-fingered gloves.

When buying sailing gloves it's a common mistake to select ones that are too snug, particularly if you are trying them on in the winter or in an air conditioned store. You'll be cursing the merchant who fitted you when you spend a half hour pulling at your fingers to remove the gloves off your sweaty hands on a hot summer day when you need to use the head. Tight-fitting gloves will painfully crush any rings you wear against your fingers when you are handling lines. I've learned to buy gloves that fit comfortably, or are even a bit loose. Sailing gloves are normally unisex items, but there are some specifically made for women. They are hard to find, but will give you the best fit.

DECK SHOES ARE A MUST

In warm weather there's a tendency to go barefoot, and what a wonderful feeling that is. We're all guilty of yielding to the temptation. However, when you are navigating the decks of a moving boat, going shoeless can mean stubbed toes and tripping the lines fantastic. Shoes are a necessity for jumping onto a dock from your boat when coming into a slip. And, beware of walking barefoot on wooden docks—splinters are never fun to remove.

Boat shoes have squeegee-like soles with small ridges that grab onto slippery surfaces and protect feet from trips and bumps. Styles range from sneakers and sandals to the traditional leather boat shoe, a staple in my shoe wardrobe. These shoes are unique in that they can get soaking wet yet are still comfortable to wear. They dry soft, retain their shape, and never seem to wear out. They may be the most comfortable shoes you'll ever own. For summer, I also like boat-soled sport sandals. Their white soles don't mark the deck and the Velcro strap keeps them securely on my feet.

Wearing leather-soled shoes, clunky sport or hiking sneakers, and stocking-covered feet is even more treacherous than going barefoot. These types of footwear have no traction on slick fiberglass, particularly if it is wet. Test shore footwear on your boat's topside for slip resistance before you wear it under way. When you invite nonboater friends for a sail, remember to suggest they pack some sort of non-skid rubber-soled shoes to wear aboard your boat.

PART FIVE

Venturing Into Outer Space

YOU AND YOUR CREW are at anchor. It's a clear night. So clear it looks like someone sprinkled stars all over the sky. Your boat undulates under your bodies as you lay topside on the bow. Every so often you feel the gentle tug of the anchor rode, promising it will hold tonight. Filled with the euphoria of a sparkling evening, you burst into song. First you hum, then you sing out loud and clear. Just you and the stars. Someone starts a song and all of you finish it, making up the words you don't remember. After a while, your repertoire runs dry and the first person yawns, then the second. It's berth time. You stand up and look around and realize that you are alone. Every other boat has pulled up anchor and departed.

The wonder of the evening becomes the dawn of the new day. The early morning air is crisp, the water silent. An engine thrums in the distance. It's time to get up and go sailing.

CHAPTER

17

Look Before You Leap

KNOWLEDGE IS POWER

This is reward time but it, too, has its moments. Now you have to use the information you learned in boating classes and from reading nautical books last winter. Don't be content to just sit in the cockpit, watching the scenery and working on your tan. When an unexpected weather front rolls in or the seas suddenly change, you and your captain will need to work together. You may not always agree on the same course of action, but that's why it's important to understand what's going on. Someday, you may have to take charge of the entire boat in an emergency. It's critically important that you:

- ○ understand the rules of the road
- ○ know how to operate your boat
- ○ learn to work in harmony with your captain
- ○ learn to read charts and plot courses
- ○ be aware of the challenges of your trip and plan adequate food, drink, and clothing
- ○ carefully consider the weather and sea conditions before setting out
- ○ tell someone where you are going

Feeling confident is important. Build your sailing self-esteem by getting educated. Learn simple boat handling strategies and why and when precautions are in order. If your captain is the strong, in-control type like mine is, the feeling of security he exudes could prompt you to rely on him too much. Ask me, I know. I used to be (and sometimes still am) content to sit back, relax, and be the go-fetcher. I seldom took the helm, or any major responsibility for that matter, so I always felt incapable—a common scenario amongst first mates who don't take a full share of the load. Once we realized what was happening, my husband made a special effort to get me involved. He even relinquishes the helm to me now and then and insists I navigate a few hairy passages.

I recommend you begin by learning the basics. The U.S. Power Squadron offers a fine program for beginning to advanced boaters, where you can become familiar with nautical terms, boat safety techniques, and beginning piloting. Many boat insurance companies offer slightly reduced rates to those who take recognized boating classes, and the information you acquire may one day save your lives. Several sailing organizations offer onboard instruction that is specifically designed for women. They are wonderful for building self-assurance and skill.

> SHE SAID: *"Aren't we there yet? It's getting dark."*
> HE SAID: *"Just a few more hours. "*

Being in the know also gives you the edge on what the captain has in store for a trip. There will almost always be times when he will withhold important information like anticipated weather changes or the true length of your trip. Wouldn't you like to know if it's going to be a rough ride, or if those "few hours" he said the trip would take might easily stretch to ten? If you understand a little about the weather, can read a chart, and know your boat's average cruising speed, you will be much better informed in any situation and able to intelligently discuss an alternate plan. I usually do my own quick estimate of timing before we leave. This is how I do it.

TRAVEL TIME = MILES ÷ SPEED

Be very conservative in estimating your boat's speed. When motoring, don't assume that you will do so at maximum potential speed; when sailing, don't assume that you'll be able to travel in a straight line with no need for tacking back and forth.

To determine travel time, you divide the distance to be traveled by this conservative speed estimate. I figure the mileage by reviewing the charts for our sailing area. We travel buoy to buoy, so it's a simple matter of determining which buoys we will pass, then "connecting the dots." I write down the distances between buoys and add any other figures (mileage from our marina to the first buoy, for example) together to estimate the mileage. It may sound more complicated than it is, but many chart books show the mileage of popular routes, as well as the magnetic compass courses.

Once I know the estimated miles we will travel and our average boat speed, the rest is simple arithmetic. For example:

10 nautical miles at 5 knots will take 2 hours

(miles ÷ speed = travel time)

My calculation is a simplified "guesstimate" that excludes the strength and direction of any wind and current we may encounter, all of which may help or hinder our progress. For example, if we are sailing against a 5-knot current and our boat's speed is 5 knots, we will feel movement (from the motion of the water running past our hull), but are going nowhere fast. Beating, or sailing directly into a stiff wind, slows forward progress as well. Determining the tactical strategies for countering natural tidal and seasonal elements is part of the challenge and fun of boating.

Reading, taking boating courses, and time on the water will help you develop these skills. It's important to remember that *you* are your captain's best aid to navigation. Your combined skills and team effort will not only make boating challenging and fun for you both, but will take a heap of stress off that guy you love.

PLANNING YOUR TRIP

Caution is your credo, and if it isn't, it should be. We all make mistakes. A good way to remember the problems as well as the fun of boating is to keep a daily trip journal. I'm not talking about the ship's log—this is your own record, whether it's a spiral notebook or a fancy bound journal. Start with the date, information about the weather conditions, time of departure, arrival, and an accounting of sea and wind conditions along the way. Record favorite restaurants and shopping locales and don't forget to note the name of the market that was responsible for ruining your barbecue with its over-the-hill chicken.

It's common to repeat visits to favorite spots year after year, particularly if you remain at the same home port. As you get more and more boating seasons under your hull, you'll begin to notice trends in the weather and sea patterns. For example, in the Mystic, Connecticut, area, May and June tend to be foggy. Our most consistently good sailing conditions are in July and early August. But by mid-August on Long Island Sound—watch out! That's when hurricane season begins. The winds get erratic, the tides go nuts, and storms brewing down south bring us large swells and fringe rains. A glance at your journal will refresh your memory about conditions the previous year and provide a valuable first step in planning when and where to cruise.

Check Guides and Charts

When setting out on a trip, part of your planning should include a cruise through the waterway guide for the area you'll be sailing. This handy book will provide you with valuable information on a specific harbor, such as potential obstructions, entry detail, whether it is a safe and comfortable anchorage, and the availability of mooring and dock facilities. Accommodation and cost information is available for all the coves, marinas, and anchorages in popular sailing areas. Getting a slip at a marina works just like going to a hotel. You often need reservations well in advance for popular harbors, especially during holiday weekends like Memorial Day, Fourth of July, and Labor Day. Moorings and anchorages are normally on a first-come, first-served basis.

Nothing ever stays the same in the world of boats, though, and the first sign that it's time to replace your waterway guide is when you find markers missing or encounter buoys that aren't on your chart. We replace our guides at least every two years. Facilities, rates, and radio call signs change. Get new charts and stay posted on changes to your sailing area by reviewing U.S. Coast Guard newsletters. Your local U.S. Power Squadron can tell you how to get on the mailing list.

Listen to the Weather Report

There are times both at anchor and under way when the weather is so erratic that you'll swear you're on an Outward Bound experience, particularly if daily conditions vary wildly, like ours do. In New England we experience several weather fronts per day. Keep abreast of what's coming your way by routinely checking weather and sea conditions in your sailing area. The marine radio weather report is updated about four times a day; listen to it. And don't forget to check your journal to see what the weather was like last year.

Many a weekend we've spent sitting at the dock tossing a volley of expletives at ourselves for canceling our plans. The marine forecast predicted doom and we missed an absolutely gorgeous sailing day. No one ever knows what the weather will do, of course, so make your best assessment before setting out by consulting several sources. Listen to the local radio station. Look outside. Learn to read the sky. Note the shape of the clouds and the direction the front is moving. Is it going your way? If you decide to take a chance when the odds for a great sail are against you, make it an educated one and know what you are doing.

Foggy Days

Fog can be beautiful over the water—as long as you don't have to sail into it. Here in New England, fog is a fact of life. Setting out in the gray matter is a gutsy thing to do, even for old-timers like us. I remember once trying to discourage a young couple, who were fairly new to boating, from embarking on a 10-hour passage in fog late one night. Fog is bad enough during the day when at least there's a chance that it will burn off, but at night, it seriously reduces visibility.

Fog is a cloud at the earth's surface that is composed of tiny condensed water droplets suspended in the air. Sailing in fog is eerie. You feel isolated because fog not only blocks vision, it muffles sound. It's as if the sky dropped a white shroud over everything except that small circle of water surrounding you and your boat. The really scary thing is that, although you feel alone, you're probably not. Other boats, ships, and obstacles may be all around you . . . somewhere. Objects such as buoys and other boats seem

larger than life when they suddenly loom up in front of you, seemingly out of nowhere. When sailing in fog, get all hands—and
eyes—on deck. The more eyes on the job, the quicker you'll be able
to divert your boat from a close encounter.

In New England waters we've come to expect seasonal fog
early in the day during spring and fall, when there is a large vari-
ance between the water and air temperatures. Although it's typical
for seasonal fog to burn off by late morning as the day warms, it
sometimes doesn't happen and we're left sailing the day in a blanket of white. Isolated land masses—islands—are more subject to
fog than larger land masses. If you're experiencing light fog at
your marina, you can normally expect it to thicken as you go
oceanward.

Learn to travel in fog. Keep your chart handy and mark each
leg of your course, noting the compass (magnetic) course between
buoys. Maintain your course and crosscheck your location as you
proceed by comparing the ocean depth on your chart to your
depthsounder measurement. The charted water along your course
is a good indicator as to whether you are where you are supposed
to be, or are seriously off course.

Monitor the marine VHF radio in case another boat is trying to
issue a warning. Friends of ours sailing in dense fog avoided colliding with a ferry because the ferry captain hailed them on the
VHF after seeing them on his radar screen. Keep an air horn handy
in the cockpit to warn oncoming boats of your presence. Its shriek
is hard to ignore and will pierce any fog. A ship's bell is good as a
continual means of shouting your position if you are anchored in
fog. (It also looks nice mounted belowdecks when it's not needed.)

If you are fortunate to have radar on your boat, it will help you
spot approaching vessels or obstructions—but know that radar
sees an object as just an object; it can't distinguish between a lobster
pot or a boat. Radar indicates an object's location and relative size,
and tracks its movement. The disadvantage of most radar systems
is that the controls are often belowdecks, leaving the helmsman
alone to spot the object the person below is telling him or her to
avoid. The person below usually has the better deal because he or
she can call the signals without experiencing the fear or foul conditions of being at the helm. On one occasion, a female friend was
manning the helm in a thunderstorm when her husband, who was

belowdecks, shouted, "Let go of the wheel if lightning strikes!" Now that's a scary thought.

Waterproof radar units are now available and allow better management in fog or storms because two people can remain on deck to navigate. We recently converted our unit to a waterproof one and love the convenience of being able to use radar where we need it most.

USE COMMON SENSE

If the weather is deteriorating or a storm is in the make, do you really need to leave? This is supposed to be "pleasure" boating. Education and experience are the only ways to combat that syndrome. Like children learning a new game, you and your captain will live through a few harrowing experiences whether you plan them or not. Many men gravitate to adventure. The very thing I love about them is their sense of machismo. But the swagger that says, "I can conquer the world" has a down side. There might be times when your captain will insist on setting sail, when common sense and a look at the sky says to stay home. (This trait is akin to men's innate stubbornness in refusing to stop for directions.)

With basic boating education behind you both, this sense of daring can offer an opportunity to build confidence in sailing in adverse conditions. The weather is iffy, but you set sail anyway and find yourselves plopped into a fog bank or a squall. It's scary at first, but you pool your knowledge and work together to get to your destination, where you arrive like survivors, both exhilarated and relieved. You've developed the skill and assurance to meet your next challenge, and will be fine tuning your combined boating expertise for years. And, you will collect enough stories to keep your friends entertained for many winters.

As your sailing experience matures, your accumulation of experiences becomes your basis for common sense. You will learn to intelligently assess a situation and to plan for it. An uncomfortable or dicey sail may not be the most pleasant you've experienced, but it has taught you how to handle adversity. More importantly, you have gained the confidence that you and your crew will arrive safely at your destination.

* * *

As you'll soon discover, the biggest problem in weekend, coastal sailing is that most of us have jobs to get to on Monday. Long weekends are the anchors of our summers. The need to get back home by Sunday evening can put a crunch on enjoyment when a storm system or fog bank has rolled in, or small craft warnings have been issued. The sensible thing to do is to delay leaving for a day and call in sick to work pleading the "blue flu." But most often, you will attempt the trip.

If you do experience a storm while you are away from your home port, bear in mind that, after a storm passes, the clear skies that it brings are often accompanied by hefty winds—and boisterous seas. Factor extra layover days into your vacations so you won't feel obligated to navigate 10-foot seas to get home. If you must set out, wear your life jackets and secure gear belowdecks. Batten down anything flapping.

On one memorable Sunday, we left Block Island in drizzle and sailed into a severe thunderstorm. It was raining so hard we could barely see land. Lightning flashed all around us. The only positive thing about the trip was that the seas weren't angry, just the sky. Suited up in our foul-weather gear, our insides stayed dry but it was a long "few hours." Eating lunch or using the head was nearly impossible, and our soaking selves brought gallons of water into the boat with each trip belowdecks, making it treacherously slippery. We learned a lesson in self-control that day.

We felt like we'd traveled for days by the time we tied onto our mooring ball. Dripping wet, we faced the task of vacating the four of us and a weekend's worth of luggage in a dinghy. We kept our duffels dry by encasing them in large green trash bags for the trip to shore. We headed gratefully for hot showers, changed into dry clothes (and reused the trash bags for our wet duds), and scooted to a nearby restaurant for lunch and stiff drinks. Trips like that are unforgettable, all right.

CHAPTER

18

Getting Under Way

COMPANY'S COMING!

Be proactive. A small bit of planning and organizing before a sail goes a long way toward keeping everyone aboard comfortable and safe. Who will be sailing with you? How long will you be sailing? Will you need any meals or snacks? Can you produce something besides peanuts and Coke for dinner if your docking plans change? How many cushions will you need to unearth to locate warm jackets? Are you equipped if it gets cold or rainy? Are life preservers for everyone nearby? Is everything stowed? Mentally review these questions before you set out to avoid unnecessary hassles while under way.

There's nothing more wonderful, or more frightening, than sharing a day on your boat with non-boating family and friends. And don't we owe it to them after they've tolerated our boat chatter all winter? If they are friends you wish to keep, take care of them and do your homework. Find out who and how many will be joining you and be sure not to exceed the capacity of your boat. It's all too easy for the numbers to mount when you invite two couples to sail with you and forget to include yourselves. The cockpits on most average-sized sailboats don't accommodate more than six people without restricting their movements or forcing some people to go forward, or elsewhere on the boat, to make some space. This can turn into a problem when the weather or sea state become adverse and all these extra people are forced to go belowdecks—not a great place to be for the weak of stomach.

Begin conditioning your family and friends for their visit by defining your version of casual to them. It's not uncommon for company to arrive in linen blazers, dresses, slippery-soled leather shoes, high heels, or those dastardly black rubber-soled shoes that leave stubborn streaks on the white parts of your boat. Don't laugh. This happens more often than I care to say. Insist that guests wear boat shoes or other rubber-soled footwear to protect them from injuring themselves and from marring your boat.

Also, it's always at least 10 degrees cooler and a bit windier by the water than it is on shore, so suggest that guests pack long pants and a light jacket or sweatshirt, even if the weather promises to be scorching hot. Finally, it won't hurt to remind them to bring sunglasses, hats, and sunscreen. Unless they're beach bums, they may not be prepared for the intensity of the sun or wind they'll be experiencing.

Discreetly inquire about motion tolerance. If your guests have never been on a boat before, or are not sure if they are susceptible to seasickness, plan to make this first sail a short one. Otherwise, you may end up swabbing the decks while feeling mighty guilty about not being able to get those pea green faces onto dry land *tout de suite.*

When guests ask what they can bring, be honest about what you need. After all, you are not running a restaurant. Let them bring their favorite beverages, salads, or baked goods, but be frank about the amount and type of storage space you have. On a small boat, excess coolers, unwieldy plastic bowls without sealing covers, and anything large made of glass can be stowage nightmares.

The scariest dish we ever enjoyed under sail was a layered Mexican dip that a guest brought aboard. It was beautifully arranged on a large glass platter with no rim, and it teetered and tottered and splattered on our laps and our boat. We ate it quickly and furiously until we were down to a dirty platter that wouldn't fit in the galley sink. I finally tucked it in a trash bag and set it snug on my berth until we got ashore. On another occasion, we hosted a cooperative dinner aboard for six couples—but I didn't plan on them all bringing their own beverages and dishes to share. We had to jostle five coolers and at least five dishes of something good to eat that needed to be stowed or refrigerated.

The shape, size, and sealability of the containers in which well-meaning visitors pack homemade potato salad, gooey brownies, and iced tea are important. Ask them to save that luscious chocolate cream pie that requires refrigeration until their next visit to your home, unless you plan to attack it soon after their arrival. Such delicate foods require too much babying for this occasion. Most people coming for the day will bring their own cooler stocked with contributions to the party, so plan in advance where you might stow it so it won't be in the way.

CONSIDER YOUR GUESTS' CAPABILITIES

Most active, healthy adults can physically manage to board a boat and maneuver about on it. But what can we do about our dear elderly relatives or friends who aren't as spry or those who have leg, back, or other injuries that handicap their movement? They too, will ask, "When are we going to get a ride on this boat you are spending all your time on?"

Boating has a glamour that few can resist. It attracts all ages and types of people who want to share the experience with you. It's difficult, however, to say to someone you love, "I don't think you can manage." Although you really *do* want them to share in your joy of boating, they don't have a clue what they're in for.

So, you set a date to take them sailing, then lay awake nights trying to figure out how you're going to pull it off. How will you get them onto the boat? Once they are settled, will they be jostled too much? Will their stomachs get upset? What if it's windy or cold and they get chilled or wet? Will they be able to tolerate heeling from side to side under sail or thumping up and down if under power? What will you do if they need to use the head? Can they manage the companionway? These questions can make you cringe and regret bragging so much about your boat. But if you make the effort, you can do it. You can share a great boating experience with special people, and they will be thrilled that you cared.

Getting Nonboaters Aboard

Attack the biggest problem first—getting guests on (and off) the boat. Think ahead about the best way to do this, keeping in mind their physical condition and your dockage situation. Are you on a slip or at a mooring? For people with difficulty climbing, stooping, and keeping their balance, boarding will be easiest if the boat is secured in a stationary position at a floating dock so they can climb aboard with the fewest contortions. A small step stool or set of steps will facilitate this task. If you don't have either, perhaps a neighbor will loan you one. If your boat is not berthed at a good boarding spot, make arrangements to bring it to a better location before guests are due to arrive so they won't be left standing and waiting for you to bring the boat around. Also, you want them to feel that what you are doing is normal boarding procedure. Return to this same spot for disembarking.

If you keep your boat on a mooring, getting guests aboard from an unstable dinghy to even a gently moving boat can be difficult. The maneuver requires an intricate dance of timing and synchronization. You may have become expert at the procedure and know exactly how and where to support and balance yourself, and how to swing into the cockpit, but first-time visitors may not. Ask someone experienced to board first to guide others, and don't make a big deal about it or they will be embarrassed.

If you are on a mooring and at a marina that runs a launch service, use it to help visitors get to your boat. Boarding will be much easier because the launch will pull alongside the widest part of your boat and enable guests to easily disembark with a small hop upward. If you cannot provide elderly or slightly infirm passengers stable boarding dockside, try this method. Besides, a launch ride is pleasant. Give guests your boat's name and location, tell them where to pick up the launch, and inform them if any costs or tips are expected. (Perhaps you can be the gracious host and pre-pay for them.) Then all you have to do is sit aboard your boat with a cool drink and await their arrival.

If your boat is at dock on a fixed piling-type slip, boarding can be most difficult. Your boat will be tied to four or more surround-ing pilings, which look like telephone poles, and it will float up and down with any prevailing tides. In New England, where high and low tide can easily vary by eight feet, getting aboard at low tide can be treacherous. It's a long way down, so a quantum leap may be re-quired to bridge the gap between the dock and the boat. If this is your situation, boarding anyone who is not agile will be a problem. I suggest you locate an easier boarding dock to use, even if it means pulling up at another marina or begging space at a gas dock for a few minutes. You'd think by now that marinas would have estab-lished handicapped parking for boats!

WHAT ARE YOUR GUESTS' EXPECTATIONS?

Why do they want to go sailing? Or do they? Are they avid wannabe's who love boats but don't own one? Or do you suspect they just want to see your boat and enjoy the scenery? If you probe for this kind of information when you extend the invitation, you'll know the answers and can proceed accordingly. Take inexperi-enced guests for a short ride and see how it goes. If we are enter-taining a special needs visitor, or there are simply too many of us aboard (even though we try, it's often hard to avoid an overly full cockpit), we may opt to motor and save the activity and confusion of hoisting sails for another day.

Before you get under way, make your visitors feel at home. Take a few minutes to show them how to operate the marine toilet, and reassure them that it's perfectly normal to be nervous about using it for the first time. If going below is a problem for them be-cause they can't handle the motion or manage the companionway, assist them and make sure they are safe. Give visitors the security of assigning them a life preserver and showing them how to wear it. As a precaution, suggest they don a pair of acupressure bands unless they are certain the motion won't bother them. And lastly, ask the captain to save his showing off for an afternoon out with the guys.

Once the engine is off and the sails are flying, inexperienced or new boaters sometimes get nervous from all the scampering about when winching in lines, from the game of musical chairs that results when changing tacks, and from the shifts in heel. Most people, though, are anxious to try their hand at sailing, which is great. You can sit back, enjoy the ride, and give orders. It's important, though, to help guests who don't wish to participate in the action to feel comfortable and get situated. Seat them where they will be relatively free of sudden jolts and flying elbows, and maybe they will want to come back.

Let everyone who wishes to take a turn at the helm do so, and be sure to photograph them there. It's a real thrill to envision oneself as "captain" and in control of a vessel. Share the sights that you enjoy with your passengers. Use the binoculars to show them points of interest. Point out your position on the chart and show them where you are headed. Instill confidence that you are in control and proceeding safely. Take lots of pictures and send them to your guests later. Even if they never go sailing with you again, they will remember the day they spent with you aboard your boat and be grateful to you for giving it to them.

OH NO, THEY BROUGHT THEIR KIDS!

Be clear about your intentions to include—or not include—children when you extend an invitation. We have issued a no-kids rule after a few harrowing experiences with guests' children on our boat. First-time sailors, accompanied by the extra challenge of children, can be disastrous, especially if you are unprepared. Let's face it—children get bored easily, they are even more active and restless than usual when in a confined area, and there's no escaping a bawling child on a boat. To me, children and sailboats are a volatile combination, yet it's done all the time. If you are going to carry youngsters on your boat, be extra vigilant about safety precautions.

Supervision of children aboard any boat is important. Be clear about what kind of behavior is allowed—and what kind isn't. Set rules and enforce them. I learned this the hard way one ghastly afternoon I spent biting my tongue while friends' children proceeded to find an assortment of things to play with belowdecks that I hadn't thought of as toys. They opened and slammed shut portholes and hatches. They shared a bag of chips on our berth and left salty debris all over the bed sheets. They stopped up the water pump and clogged the head. However, the full run they had of my inner space while we were sailing was not nearly as frightening as when their antics moved topside.

Ask guests with wee ones to bring games, books, soft toys, and other quiet activities to keep their children safely entertained while they are on the boat. Some of my boating friends who often have children aboard keep a few appropriate toys on hand—just in case.

Safety is paramount. Make it a rule that children on your boat wear life jackets at all times (keep a child-sized PFD aboard). Children get rambunctious and may run where an adult would tread carefully. Child overboard drills are no fun. I cringe when I see young ones sitting up on the bow, even if they are wearing life jackets. If children on your boat wish to be up forward, have an adult go with them. Little heads are hard to find amidst big waves.

If children are frequent visitors, or they belong to you, install sturdy safety netting around your boat's lifelines and check its strength by pushing hard against it all around. Be sure it can sustain the weight of small children flinging themselves against it. A safety belt with a tether is a must for roving toddlers. Clip one end securely to the lifeline and keep a close watch on their travels.

GUESTS AND RAIN—WHAT TO DO?

It happens to everyone at one time or another. Company shows up anticipating a great day on the water, and the weather doesn't co-operate. So there you are, you and the captain, sitting belowdecks out of the wind and rain having your morning coffee and wonder-ing what to do. Guests are due soon and are expecting to go for a sail. If you have a cell phone, it's easy enough to call them and reschedule, or they can contact you (assuming the cellular network is functioning or you're within range). Otherwise, to reach a pay phone to resolve the issue means donning a full set of foul-weather gear and either taking a soggy dinghy ride into shore or a long walk up the dock. Maybe, just maybe, you will reach them before they leave home.

Oftentimes visitors show up regardless of impending bad weather. The date was on their schedule and they're not sure when they can come again. We once had a young couple insist on coming the day after a hurricane struck our area, even though there was no way we could go sailing. But we did have a lovely time. We sat in the cockpit and looked at their wedding pictures, then went out for a fine meal. In fact, we've had some of our best times with people on nonsailing days. It's kind of like sloughing off work. We have an excuse for not performing because of the bad weather, so we end up totally relaxed, enjoying a great visit.

If it's foggy, windy, or a small-craft warning type of day, we take a motor trip up the Mystic River where it is certain to be calm. Or, we'll often tie up at a town dock and stroll the main avenue be-fore returning to port. If you can devise a default trip like this for your sailing area, you'll be able to satisfy your guests with a pleas-ant ride without risk or discomfort. We keep local tour guides on our boat for days when the weather is too foul to do any boating. Sometimes we go sightseeing, but often we just hang out, keeping ourselves warm and dry inside our boat. It's not a bad way to in-troduce the boating life to people. It's far superior to being at home and much more fun.

Years ago, good friends drove down from upstate New York to join us for a weekend of sailing. Our plans to sail to Newport were foiled when small-craft warnings were issued—we sailed a 27-foot Buccaneer back then, which qualified as a borderline small craft—

so we spent a blustery weekend on our mooring. After a day of dinghying back and forth to shore under not-so-nice conditions, we canceled dinner out and instead drank red wine and ate beef stew and brown bread in our cozy cabin. We ended up having a better visit than we would have had in Newport, with no sunburn to boot.

My advice is to go with the flow. Collect ideas for entertaining those visitors you know won't be content to stay put. Sometimes I take the wives shopping while the husbands are just as happy to sit on the boat and read or take a nap. I can remember the time we convinced my dad to take the train up from Stamford for a day on the water. We should have said "in" the water. He arrived to a miserably rainy day that never quit. Luckily, we were able to turn the day into a sightseeing jaunt. We toured a submarine at Groton, hit the Mystic Aquarium, ate lunch at an Italian restaurant, then capped the day with a visit to a local winery. Dad was a tired, damp, but happy man by the time we put him on the train that evening. It does, indeed, pay to keep area brochures on board.

The important thing is to *relax*. You can't control the weather, so use the unexpected downtime to enhance your friendships and get to know your family again. Lord knows we spend enough time keeping busy and managing to avoid such pleasant experiences.

GETTING READY TO GO

Whenever you set sail, always let someone know where you are headed, when you expect to return, and how to reach you. What if there is a family emergency? Do you have a cell phone? Will you monitor a specific marine radio channel? Are you staying at a marina where the dockmaster might get a message to your boat? Don't you want someone to worry about whether or not you return?

An overdue boat is always a cause for concern. It's a big ocean. If no one knows where you were headed, a Coast Guard search will be impossible. I was very upset with my husband one glorious October weekend. He, two boating buddies, and their sons were to stay overnight at the marina to work on closing the boats for the season. But all three men, so I am told, looked at each other and said, "What are we doing here? Let's go to Block [Island]!" So they set sail on our boat and didn't return until the following day. I was appalled. There they were on the water with two young boys and not a soul knew they had left. I still haven't forgiven them for that one. We all do dumb things sometimes.

Pack Your Lunch

How I envy those lucky people who can navigate or relax below, totally unaffected by a boat's motion. Sometimes, a calm day can unexpectedly become rough, and going below (for me) is almost impossible. When I first started sailing, I waited until everyone's stomachs started growling before I'd descend to the galley, gather all the lunch fixings, slice some rolls, and make sandwiches. By the time I finished, found the chips, and made sure everyone had drinks and napkins, my belly was heaving with the boat.

I learned to prepare snacks and lunches before setting out. Rolls, long buns, or pita bread halves that can be managed in one hand are perfect for sandwiches because the other hand is usually watching a drink or grabbing for some chips. With a one-hand lunch, even the helmsman can manage to eat without leaving his post. I always wrap the pre-made sandwiches in foil because it stays put, makes its own plate, and is easily disposable. I like to stow all of the sandwiches in a plastic bag or wicker serving basket in the ice chest, and set aside drinks in a separate, easily accessible cooler that's placed either in the cockpit or a secure place below. Leave the cookies and chips where you can snag them without digging, and use a thermos to keep coffee, water (for tea or hot chocolate), or soup hot while under sail. When stomachs begin to growl, you will be ready for them. Simply go below, grab the lunch goodies, and you're done. Throw loose empties into the sink or trash and clean it all up once you dock.

Stow Everything

Most guys get a thrill out of heavy heeling and love to dip the rail, all of which plays havoc with your inner space. Make it a rule to always stow loose items before setting out. Envision the insides of your boat tipped at a 45° degree angle and seesawing from side to side, then look around. Tuck away any heavy item that you think is likely to careen across the boat under heel. Unless you plan to cook under way, lock down the gimballing on the oven to keep it from swinging back and forth. Tie down doors or drawers that fly open under pressure so they won't spill their contents. Lash down anything that will swing and clank. (We had a hanging oil lamp that had a better time than we did one trip.) Drain the sinks in the galley and head so standing water doesn't back up and gurgle over, leaving the cabin sole wet and dangerous. Plug sinks and close seacock valves, portholes, and hatches to prevent water from bubbling up or spraying into the boat. It takes a long time to dry out wet cushions, and it's downright nasty sleeping on a wet berth.

Keep the Cockpit In Order

Use plastic-zippered cases to enclose charts and then place them under the cockpit cushions to keep them out of the way. The charts will remain handy and you won't need to dash up and down the companionway to retrieve them each time the captain asks for one. If you don't own cockpit cushions, nag the captain to order some, or use flotation cushions. Unless you've got ample padding of your own, you'll find that cockpit seating gets harder as a trip progresses.

Tie a small plastic bag somewhere in the cockpit—perhaps in a locker or cubby—to stow trash, empty soda cans, and other small items that are likely to fly around when you tack. Secure beverages by using gimbaled drink holders or nonskid cozies. I've found that wide-bottomed cups with lids are great, as long as they have tight-fitting lids and aren't ceramic.

CHAPTER

19

Under the Sail

WHAT DID YOU SAY?

It's a beautiful day and you're at the helm enjoying the cool breeze on your face when *somebody yells!* You snap to attention and realize you are headed for a reef. Quickly recovering your course, you steer to safety while the captain continues his tirade. He's calling you names he hasn't used for you since you wallpapered the dining room together. You shout back a retort, then spend the rest of the trip sulking and figuring out ways to make him grovel in apology later on.

This scenario happens to the best of us women sailors all the time. Look around and notice how many couples pulling into dock after a sail are not speaking to each other. Overactive shouting from our male counterparts is most prevalent amongst new boatowners. The experienced captains are all yelled out.

A captain's insecurity about reaching a destination without wrecking the boat or having someone injured often gets transferred to the person he loves the most. You. Don't take it personally. Be calm, understand the situation, and respond quickly and as best you can to his concern. You can plan your payback once you've bypassed the problem—argue about who is right later. As you gain sailing experience, the two of you will become a well-oiled sailing machine that operates in near perfect harmony. The yelling fits will subside. Do as he asks, as long as it's reasonable.

There is, of course, a longstanding tradition of a captain's word being law. On commercial ships, this is indeed the case. No court will acquit anyone who disobeys a direct ship handling order. On a family vessel, however, one hopes that decisions about navigation, sail handling, and the like are reached by mutual consensus. Still, everyone on board must recognize that, in emergencies, when the ship is threatened, and fast action is critical, someone must be in charge—no questions asked. That person is the captain.

Onboard communication problems can occur for many reasons, including too much knowledge. The winter we bought our first boat, we signed up for any boating class offered. I had never been on a boat before, so my captain figured that classroom learning would make me an instant expert. I'll never forget our first time on the water. With a flourish, we got our brand-new 27-foot Buccaneer off the dock. It was smooth motoring until my captain decided to hoist the sail. Unfortunately, I had yet to connect the terms halyard, shroud, and mainstay with the ropes in my hand, so I wasted critical time figuring out what he was asking me to do. We jibed; it wasn't pleasant; and I was blamed. We had our first of many nautical fights.

HE SAID: *"Tweak the Cunningham."*

SHE SAID: *"Do you mean you want me to pull on this rope over here?"*

Do learn to use sailing jargon, but be certain that the person it is directed at knows what you are talking about. Take it slow. Fancy words won't get you there any faster or help you enjoy your trip any better. Although nautical terms are important to understand and learn, they shouldn't be used at the expense of good communication.

THE HELM HOG

The captain's ship is his baby. He is happiest when planted at the helm barking orders. Often, it will be just the two of you aboard and you will be the captain's number one lackey. Letting out the genoa, tightening the mainsail, or dashing below to grab him a drink or warm jacket all falls to the person *not* at the helm. At the end of a heavy sailing day you may feel like you've just run a marathon, while your captain, who has plunked himself at the helm the entire time, is invigorated. If you've got a knee injury or any other excuse not to scurry about, the captain may be forced to relinquish the helm to you. And then you'll find out his secret. Handling the helm isn't as hard as he professes.

When I got my first few turns at the helm, my captain acted like a proud father who's allowing someone else to hold his baby.

He prowled the decks tweaking the lines, seeking perfection. When sailing in light air or wing-and-wing, he stood on deck holding the lower edge of the genoa erect with the tip of the boathook. He shifted our point of sail, then chastised me for allowing the sails to luff. I quickly learned to be alert to shifts of all kinds—natural ones from the wind and water, and induced ones from my honey's tampering. Ever since our first sail when I accidentally jibed the mainsail, nearly capsizing my captain, I have remained apprehensive whenever anyone, particularly he, leaves the safety of the cockpit to go forward. So whenever anyone is stalking the decks, be alert. Keep the helm steady, on course, and on the proper tack.

Can You Save Your Captain?

Could you save your captain if he fell overboard? Pester him to wear a life preserver. Learn how to single-handedly operate your boat's recovery devices. Most boaters find the Lifesling system valuable because it enables one person to haul another back onto a boat by using the leverage of a winch. If you have one aboard, read the directions and understand how it operates. Whenever someone's hat or other article blows overboard, take advantage of the situation to practice quick recovery procedures. Stop the boat and go back for the hat. It could be you, it could be him.

HANDLING HEELING

I've been sailing for almost 20 years now and I still can't get used to hard heeling; that is, when a boat is tipped over so far that water slurps over the coaming and onto the boat, and the sails are so low in the water that they may be scooping some up, too. The best place to be in these conditions is on the high side of the cockpit because it's the driest (but also the scariest).

I embarrassed my captain a few years ago when we were testing a new center cockpit sailboat. Our dauntless dealer was at the helm and, like many men, I knew he was showing off as he held the boat at close to a 45° heel. On a center cockpit boat (also called a wedding cake), the cockpit sits higher than on an aft cockpit boat (like we normally sailed), which means that the water is farther away. When I did my usual chicken-style scamper to the high side, I found myself looking straight into the water, which appeared to be at least 20 feet down. So I did what any decent woman would do. I screamed shamelessly. My husband still can't figure out what happened and the boat dealer didn't care. We bought the boat.

When you find yourself on the high side and ready to scream in bloody terror, you will feel more secure if you brace your feet firmly against the opposite side of the boat. Grab a stanchion from behind and hold on tight. If the captain asks you to tend to a line on the low side, try to pawn the job off on another crewmember because it will be difficult to get there. If the helmsman cannot see under the sail, it's important for a crewmember to be seated on the low side to alert the captain to what's ahead. Wearing life jackets is essential, especially during wild rides. A good rule when maneuvering around the boat when under way, regardless of conditions, is to keep at least one hand holding onto the boat, and as much of your body as low and close to the topsides as possible.

This is probably as good a time as any to admit that I don't swim. I panic whenever my feet can't touch the water's bottom and then flap my arms around in an anxiety attack until I get exhausted and someone takes pity on me. Nevertheless, I've always felt safe on our boat because I am up and away from the water. I seldom get wet, except if it's raining. I guess I also should confess that heights make me squeamish. So you see, even if you have a few hang-ups like I do, you can still enjoy boating. Just respect the water and take safety precautions.

DON'T ORDER DINNER ON THE VHF RADIO

I get very annoyed when trying to contact a marina to discuss docking arrangements and having to wait my turn because the airways are clogged with nonsensical conversations. Last summer I tried to contact a dockmaster and had to wait 10 minutes while two women exchanged recipes over the VHF. Do I sound incensed? I am. With cell phones everywhere, there is often no longer a need to conduct personal conversations on the marine radio. But if you do, please remember to keep conversations short and, above all, to talk only on the appropriate channels—certainly not channels 9 or 16.

All VHF radio talk is simplex, which means that two people cannot speak at the same time. Therefore, if you wish to use the radio you must wait until a break in conversation or you will be unable to communicate. All mariners should respect the marine radio—it is a form of vital communication—and understand its usage protocol. Channels 16 and 9 are the officially designated (by the Federal Communications Commission) hailing channels, restricted to short informational calls. Use channel 16 to make initial contact with a marina or another vessel, but once the communication is established, switch to another mutually agreed frequency to continue the discussion.

Technology is bringing more communication alternatives to the waterways—even laptop computers are showing up on board to send and receive e-mail and faxes. It's getting increasingly difficult to get away from the outside world. What a pity.

THE WIND IN YOUR HAIR IS THE WAY IT'S BLOWING

To this day, one of my major problems as a sailor is figuring out which direction the wind is coming from. Either I'm obtuse, or I have one of those female defects that men brag about. When I put my hand to the ends of my hair, people I sail with think I'm either waving or preening. I'm really testing the wind. It works for me.

The most common device for finding wind direction is called, cleverly enough, a wind direction finder. It looks like a weather vane and sits high atop a mast. Forget about it helping you. You'll get a stiff neck trying to look up at it, and if you happen to be at the helm, you're liable to crash into something because you're not watching where you're going.

For me, a better way to figure out wind direction is to look at the telltales on our boat. Telltales are "strings," (they're often pieces of yarn) about 10 inches long that are attached either to sails or shrouds (wire supports that keep the mast upright). When affixed to sails, they indicate whether or not the sails are trimmed properly (which is, of course, directly related to wind direction). A more direct indication of wind direction is the telltales that are affixed to shrouds. The direction of their streaming tells you how far off the bow or beam the wind is.

Jibs with telltales often have up to three sets, placed at the top, middle, and bottom near the forward edge. When the sails are perfectly trimmed for your course, the telltales on all sets are streaming horizontally. When they're not, sail trim is called for. Learning how to read telltales on sails is an art that all sailors should master.

My favorite instrument, a wind direction indicator, is typically mounted in the cockpit alongside the speed and depth indicators. On its circular face is an aerial outline of a boat, as seen from above, with directional markings notched all around the perimeter. The indicator needle points to the direction of the wind relative to your boat's orientation to the wind. For example, if the wind is directly behind you, the needle will point to the stern of the boat. With that wind direction, you could sail wing-and-wing, one of the prettiest points of sail to look at and the hardest to maintain. To keep the sails filled, you just have to keep the indicator needle pointed toward the stern—easier said than done.

Optimum wind direction for sailing close hauled and on a reach are pre-scored on the dial. Just keep the needle pointed within the appropriate ranges and you'll look like an expert sailor, even if you can't tell from which direction the wind is blowing.

Along with wind speed and direction, water conditions and tidal changes also affect the progress of a sailboat. Unless you're making course changes or setting your sails, flapping, or luffing, sails can be a sign of trouble. When the wind is not pushing sails out firmly, boat speed is diminished and it becomes difficult to stay on course. The wind is your engine. Sail trim and steering are your controls.

No matter what type of boat you have, hands-on experience is the best way to learn how it responds to varying conditions. The bigger the boat, the more forgiving. If you're having a rough go of it, consider taking a class that offers hands-on training. The helmsman and crew need to work in harmony to achieve the sail set and course that will provide the most comfortable means of making headway on their cruise.

Maintaining the Helm

Once the sails are set properly and you are at the helm, make note of the compass course you are on and look ahead for a point of reference—it can be a prominent point of land, a buoy, or even a cloud for a while—but beware of using a point of reference that moves quickly. If you keep to this course and head for the mark you have chosen, the sails will stay filled until the wind or water conditions change. After you get the feel of the wheel or tiller, and the sails are properly trimmed, keeping on course will seem effortless because the boat will be perfectly balanced.

When the wind becomes gusty and the waves more aggressive, you will need to keep rebalancing the helm to keep the boat on course. You will always bounce around less if the mainsail is up, even if you're motoring, because the sail acts as a fulcrum and lowers the center of gravity.

LOOK OUT BELOW

If you think that maneuvering about a boat at dock is tough, wait until you try it under way. A companionway is a hole in your boat you should respect. Those skinny space-saving ladder-types can be treacherous. The safest method to get below is to descend backwards, as if you were stepping down a ladder. Even then, you'll never know what evils the avid sailors in the cockpit are planning. Could it always be coincidence that when someone goes below is exactly the time the captain must haul up a sail or try a trick maneuver? Once belowdecks, you will be subject to the roll of the waves and wakes of passing powerboats, so always hold on and walk low and slow. Wear rubber-soled shoes for traction. You'll appreciate all the help you can get.

Make sure there are plenty of strategically placed handholds down below on your vessel; you can buy extras at any marine store. Don't, however, defeat their purpose by mounting them at eye or head level, or wherever else they will protrude and cause injury. In the head, handholds can double as towel racks and still act as braces to prevent people from banging their heads or other body parts should the boat lurch. Remember the story I told earlier about the friend who came barreling out of the head door, toilet seat and all, when the captain had to tack without warning? Maybe we should devise a cockpit-to-head-signal that can warn people to hold on. How about a buzzer system? We recently installed a cockpit radio that is equipped with an intercom that could easily work as a warning system. Now the helmsman only need remember to use it.

There's always an easier way to perform a task on board. Sailing books and classes provide great how-to information, but you will still need to adapt that knowledge to your own abilities and levels of fitness, coordination, and experience. Here are a few things that work for me.

Are You the Wench on the Winch?

Winches on sailboats are used to hoist and adjust sails. The most important thing I can tell you about them is to keep your hands, face, and feet out of the way when unfurling any line from a winch, especially when it's tightly coiled. When releasing a jib sheet, for example, stand back a bit and unwrap the line upward, flinging it outward and away from you as it releases. If you need to let the line out just a bit to adjust the sail set, do so slowly, always keeping at least one wrap of the line coiled at around the winch. Use the security of the winch as a lever in releasing a tight line. There will be a tremendous pull on that line, so be very careful to avoid catching your fingers between the coils. The result is painful. Never grab a line that the wind is pulling taut and allow it to slip through your hands, or you'll get a nasty rope burn, even if you are wearing gloves.

When sailing, the bitter, or unattached, ends of the genoa, jib and mainsail sheets typically end up as heaps in the cockpit. Keep them unknotted, free to run, and flaked in a neat pile so they will be ready to be released. I like to stash the mainsail lines under the end of a cockpit cushion. They are a little lumpy to sit on, but they remain out of the way and are ready to be released when it's time to lower the sail. The genoa or jib sheets should be coiled and neatly placed below the winch on which they are to be used. When working with the lines, make sure no one is stepping on them, sitting on them, or chewing on them.

To perform winching duties safely and comfortably, I usually kneel over the winch and brace myself as best I can. I also like to keep a cushion handy to kneel on. No matter how you do it, chances are that your knees and shins will be pretty banged up by the end of a trip if you've done some scrambling around.

Sailing Attire

Even when other men join us for a sail and I don't expect to help
with the lines, I leave my sailing gloves on so I'm always ready to
pitch in when needed. As the first mate, I'm actively climbing up
and down the companionway, kneeling over a winch, and contorting in the usual unladylike positions that are part of sailing. My
gloves have saved my hands from a multitude of scrapes and cuts.

Sailing attire can be summed up in two words: loose and comfortable. This is not the time to wear shorts that are tight or real
short, let alone anything else that's restrictive or revealing. Shorts
or long pants that are difficult to get on or off can be a problem
when using the head under way. Leggings, biker shorts, sweats,
long T-shirts, bathing suits, and any clothes with elastic waistlines
all qualify as winners. Save your sexy clothes for when you're
through sailing for the day.

Don't Overdo the Fluids

Drink enough fluids to keep from dehydrating, but not so much
that you are beating a constant path to the head. Using the head
under heavy sailing conditions is for the brave, stupid, or desperate.
Getting undressed and redressed in a tiny, heaving, airless space
can be treacherous when you are trying to hang on to the boat with
one hand and pull up your pants with the other. A trivial fact that
might make you feel better about the ease with which men can relieve themselves on a boat: statistics show that the most common
cause of accidental drowning among men on boats is from. . . . Yep,
you guessed it!

A Few Basics You Don't Want to Learn the Hard Way

- Port is the boat's left; starboard is the boat's right.
- The "boom" is called "boom" for a good reason. Keep your
  head down.
- Stay away from anything bigger than your boat, like a barge.
- The words "passage" and "gut" are nautical terms for tricky,
  so pay attention.

○ Don't run over lobster pots and fish traps. They are always where you don't want them to be and will bring your trip to a screeching halt when they tangle in your prop.
○ Keep out of the way of flying lines and helpful elbows.
○ Wear shoes when under way.
○ Don't dangle your feet overboard.
○ Wear a U.S. Coast Guard certified PFD (life jacket).

The Wind Stole Your Words

Trying to communicate on a boat when one person is on the bow and the other is at the helm, is a real challenge if the wind is blowing away from the person who's trying to hear. Usually, that person won't be able to hear a word being said. Many times, I've been needlessly blamed for not following orders when I just didn't hear them. The captain's roar diminishes to a whisper, and it's your fault for missing the mark he was yelling about.

A good sailing team agrees in advance on a few hand signals to use when verbal communication is difficult. Thumbs up and thumbs down are universal. Crossed arms usually mean stop, and pointing to port or starboard alerts the helmsman to changes in steering direction or perhaps an obstacle. You don't, however, want to use hand signals if you are racing! If your opponents are close enough to you, they are perfectly capable of reading common hand signals, too. (Sailboat racing is an activity I've learned to avoid. It can become so serious that it ceases to be fun, so I let the racers do their thing while I spend the day at the beach.)

To describe the location of an object or obstacle, or the direction the helmsman needs to steer, it's more precise to use the "clock method" to communicate than hand signals. It's easy. Pretend that your boat is the face of a clock. If an object is at 3:00, it is directly abeam; at 12:00, it is dead on; at 1:00 it is a few points off your starboard bow.

RED RIGHT RETURNING

"Red right returning" is a common way many boaters are taught to remember to leave red buoys to starboard when coming into port. This rule works great as long as you can figure out if you are truly returning. Sometimes you may perceive yourselves as entering a port only to find that you are actually exiting through a channel into another harbor, which means that the red buoys should be left to port. Innocent mistakes like this can put your boat aground in shallow channels or damaged by rocks, wrecks, or whatever else that red buoy marks. For this reason it is important to keep a chart handy and use it to determine which side of a red buoy guarantees safe passage.

COMING INTO PORT

You've had an exhilarating sail. Now, it's time to go home. Unless you've taken over the helm, or have another agile crewmember aboard, you are the onboard docking attendant. Depending on whether you'll be pulling into a slip, picking up a mooring, or dropping an anchor, you'll have to set up the lines and fenders on the correct side of the boat, get out the boathook, prepare the anchor and anchor rode, or pray.

These procedures aren't so bad once you get the hang of them.

Coming into a Slip

This maneuver can be a real fire drill, especially if you are not familiar with the marina or slip you are entering. If that's the case, call ahead on the VHF radio and ask on which side you should set up your fenders and docklines. And then get moving.

Make sure you have enough docklines. You will need at least three: a bow line, a stern line, and a springline (an amidships line). Depending on the kind of slip you're taking, you may very well need a second springline and/or additional bow and/or stern lines. Therefore, it's essential to keep ready-to-use extra lines handy. After you ready the lines, make sure they are attached to your boat. Don't laugh! It's not uncommon to toss a line to someone ashore only to find that you've forgotten to cleat one end of it to your boat. Once cleated, pull the remainder of the line out and *over* the lifelines so it won't get caught as it's tossed.

The number and size of fenders you will need also depends on the kind of slip you're taking, as well as the length, weight, and overall shape of your boat.

Have all lines untangled, coiled, and ready to heave. A hefty length of line—like the bow line on our boat—may be heavy when fully coiled, especially if it is wet. I can barely lift ours, let alone toss it any distance. I've learned, however, that I do not have to throw the entire coil—instead, I simply take off a few coils from the end to toss. There will be excess line laying on the deck when you do this, so be careful not to ensnare your feet, and keep the remainder of the coil free to unfurl. With the full line, or the first few coils from the end, position yourself between midship and the bow and hope that someone spots your approaching boat and offers to take the line and help you dock.

The bigger your boat, the less frequently you'll be called upon to bring it in unassisted. Smaller sailboats, say, those less than 32 feet, usually don't require assistance under normal sea and wind conditions, unless the dock is too high or too low for disembarking. However, when a larger sailboat comes to roost, other boaters are usually quick to assist, particularly if it is headed for their dock. If you think you will need help, wave, shout, toot a horn, or find another way to attract attention as you approach. Sailboats are so

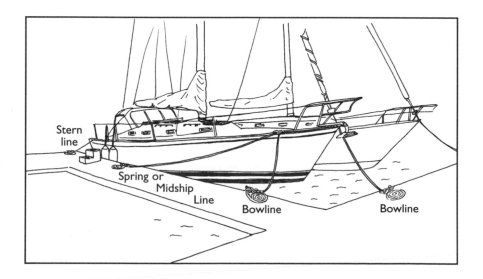

quiet that fellow mariners often aren't aware that one is slipping in until it's too late for them to help.

If you see waiting hands to assist you as you approach your slip, toss them either the springline or bow line, depending on the wind and current conditions. We always secure our springline first because it stops the forward motion of the boat. Once that is done, it's easy enough to get the bow, then stern lines out. A certain amount of piloting skill is a plus when docking a sailboat. Wind may be blowing your boat onto or off the dock. A strong current can also have a big effect on how you approach a dock. In certain situations, then, you may need to offer the stern line first. When you toss a line to someone, call out if it's the bow line, springline, or stern line so they'll know which dock cleat to wrap it around. If the stern line goes out last, the helmsman can usually handle it because the engine is in neutral and the boat is under control.

When heaving a line, toss it up and out with a slight twist, aiming as close to the waiting hands as you can. If you miss, quickly pull the line back to you. It will be wet and heavier now, so give it some extra oomph when you retoss it.

Once the boat is secure, the captain will want to recheck and redo all the lines. This is perfectly normal behavior. He will probably fuss over them for a long time, coiling the ends into flat rings. Use this time to go below and clean up yourself and the clutter from your sail.

ON YOUR OWN If you find yourself having to dock with no helping hands ashore, be aware that the difficulty increases in proportion to the size of your boat. Hopping onto the dock from a moving vessel is a feat for the fit and fleet of foot. Coordination and balance are important. Don't try this if you have any problems with your knees, legs, ankles, or feet. A poor landing can result in a myriad of sprains, twists or stubs that will ruin your trip and maybe your boating season.

Wear shoes that are sturdy enough to cushion your landing and won't fall off your feet. Assuming you are docking starboard-side-to, stand as close to the bow as you can with the springline or bow line properly cleated and coiled over your right arm. Place your feet just outside the lifelines on the outer edge of the boat as you slowly approach your slip. With your left arm, brace yourself

against a halyard or other fixed vertical line on your boat for support. When you are within a foot or two of the dock, step off. When
both feet are squarely on the dock, cleat the line to stop the boat.
Get the bow or springline line next, then the stern.

Once I got accustomed to easily pushing a small boat off the
dock or away from other boats, I failed to realize that the rules
change with larger boats. When you're fending off several thou-
sand pounds of boat, guess who's going to win? Resist the natural
temptation to fend your boat off with your foot, hand, or any
other appendage you care about—except if that boat is a small
craft. The heavier and larger the boat, the more important it is to
squelch this urge.

If you attempt to grab onto your boat's coaming to pull it toward you, be prepared to let go of it, too. The boat may surprise
you and swing away from the dock, leaving you hanging off the
lifelines with your feet in the water and feeling like a fool. I wore
wet shoes for several days after that incident. Performances such as
these are marks of new or inept boaters. Don't be surprised if your
learning experiences are peppered with the hearty chuckles of onlookers. These are the same folks who will be the first to assist if
they see that you're in trouble. Isn't the camaraderie amongst
boaters wonderful?

Picking up a Mooring

Many marinas offer moorings as alternatives to slips and, for ease
of docking, they can't be beat. Picking up a mooring is much simpler and takes less coordination and planning than pulling into a
slip. Like everything, though, it takes a bit of practice.

You will almost always need a boathook. Hand signals will
help you direct the helmsman toward the mooring buoy and let
him know if you have captured the elusive little bobber. On the
surface, moorings appear as balls or buoys; most often, you'll grab
the mooring by means of a loop that's attached to it, or by a long,
handy, pick-up stick called a pennant or mast. Most moorings
have a line already attached to them that you can bring aboard
and secure on your boat. Keep an extra line ready though, just in
case the line is too big for the cleat on your boat, or too short,
frayed, or slimy.

A mooring mast, or a pick-up pennant, enables you to grab hold of a mooring without using a boathook. It floats high enough so you can grab it with an extended arm. Lie down flat, as close to the bow of the boat as you can, and reach out for the pennant as the helmsman approaches. Haul it up onto your boat until you see the loop of the mooring line (to which it is attached), then quickly secure the mooring line around the bow cleat. It's important to be speedy while the line is slack because the boat will begin pulling away—and thereby tightening the line—once the wind catches the bow. You're on. Turn off the engine and have a cold drink. That's all there is to it.

Unfortunately, not all moorings are equipped with mooring masts, so you do have to learn the traditional method of snagging a mooring, for which a boathook is essential. The boathook acts as an extension of your arm and allows you to reach farther down to hook the mooring line. As the helmsman rounds up to the mooring, poke an extended boathook under the lowest lifeline (on some boats you will be able to reach by simply leaning over at the bow) and endeavor to hook the line just behind the float on the mooring. Try for any part of the line you can hook and quickly draw it up onto your boat, find the loop, and drape it around the bow cleat. If you miss, the helmsman will have to circle around for another swipe at it.

When picking up either kind of mooring, the helmsman's visibility is greatly reduced as the boat nears the mooring. He will depend on you to give clear directions—that's when your agreed-upon hand signals are so valuable—about the location of the mooring, its distance from you, and whether or not you've been successful at capturing it.

One caveat: It's part of the sailing tradition that, when you're first learning how to pick up a mooring, you'll do so when you're bone tired, at the end of a long, hard sail, and at cocktail hour in waters crowded with already moored or anchored boats. You are their entertainment. Enjoy being on stage!

Anchoring

Setting an anchor is trickier than picking up a mooring because if it is not done correctly your boat will drag through the water, headed for certain trouble. Lowering (and raising) an anchor is grunt work better left to anyone else you can pawn it off on. Your best chances are with unsuspecting male guests who are just learning to take orders, but any ambitious crewmember who loves to help out is fair game.

When we anchor, my captain and I swap places. I operate the helm while he goes forward and struggles with the anchor. Hand signals are very important because the helmsman must know when the anchor is down and how and when he or she needs to accelerate or stop, or go forward or reverse. While setting the anchor, your boat will not be moving in sync with vessels already anchored, so the helmsman needs to also be careful not to stray over into a neighbor's territory. Like a mooring, once the anchor is properly set, your boat will always point into the wind. (Unless there's a strong current running through the anchorage.)

Many boating classes teach the mechanics of anchoring, and many fine articles have been written on the subject. (It seems that almost every month one of the major boating magazines publishes a piece on some aspect of anchoring.) I strongly advise you and your captain to take advantage of these resources. Simply choosing a spot in a crowded anchorage among other boats is a challenge. Factors like water depth, holding ground, and whether nearby anchored boats are using chain or line, and their boats' type and size, all affect your decision. Much of this knowledge comes with practice, but it doesn't hurt to have a solid technical base before proceeding. There is so much freedom in being able to drop anchor—and it doesn't cost a silver dime.

PART SIX

At Ease

THE WATER SURFACE glistens diamonds, reflecting the dropping afternoon sun. We pull in, windblown, a little sweaty, definitely salty. A gratifying day's sail behind us, we're relaxed, renewed, and at ease. Settling in for a night on the water is the equivalent of arriving home from a rewarding day's work. We wind down, revel in our accomplishments, and share the day's adventures with our favorite people. We're now ready for the evening. Time to brag, time to dine, time to think about tomorrow's adventures.

CHAPTER

20

To the Showers

AT DAY'S END

There's nothing more active than a boat at rest, whether it's the hub-bub of activity surrounding you, a boat zipping by your mooring, or the gang congregating for cocktails on the dock outside your slip. This is also when you deal with miscellaneous, land-related tasks like taking a real shower, flushing an authentic toilet, catching up on some laundry, walking the dog, or simply restocking provisions. Concentrate on first getting the most urgent chores accomplished—not taking Fido for his constitutional could create a major mess—then curl up in your cockpit with a good novel or take a nap.

Oddly enough, the first thing that most boaters think about once we're at rest is how good a hot shower will feel (and a cold cocktail will taste). It's pitiful that what the wonderful sport of sail-ing comes down to is the overwhelming need to wash off the day's salt. We discuss our forthcoming shower with fellow boaters in avid anticipation. When we'll do it. How we'll do it. Showering takes on the aspects of a social event as we gather in herds to in-vade a marina's busy stalls. We wait in long lines, shower totes in hand, joking and talking boats.

The act of bathing is cathartic. We relive our day while the hot water rains down our backs, and sort through our thoughts as we scrub the salt out of our hair and sponge off our bodies with scented soaps. We are so caught up in the aura of bathing that we barely notice that the showers are untidy. We make do, finding the highest hook for our tote so it won't touch anything wet, and wear shower shoes so we don't step in anything gross. Marina shower rooms are often so steamy that we sweat off the effects of our bath just getting dressed. But we don't care, because we've done it. We've showered! We're renewed and refreshed. Let the party begin.

MANAGING A SHOWER AT A MARINA

Many coastal cruisers like us are at the mercy of marina shower facilities when it comes time to indulge in the luxury of bathing because our boats do not have adequate hot water or space to get clean. We learn to tolerate all manner of marina showers, from primitive wooden stalls equipped with only a shower head and clothes hook, to private tiled cubicles with curtains, shelves, and hooks. True luxury is finding electrical outlets for our hair dryers and mirrors for applying makeup.

You can expect a marina shower to be swelteringly humid and unkempt on days when there is high activity. Let's face it. People are messy. When forty or fifty people a day shower in a three-stall facility, most marinas have trouble keeping ahead of overloaded trash cans, plugged toilets, and sand-tracked or dirty tiled floors. When you encounter this situation, consider yourself lucky if there is hot water, ample toilet paper, and an operating air blower or fresh paper towels to dry your hands. Sometimes, the only clean thing in a marina's shower stall is the water streaming out of the shower head and, with a little luck, you. But like it or not, you'll learn to deal with all kinds of unpleasant facilities and still crave that refreshing shower like the rest of us goof balls.

Make the process of using a marina shower as easy as possible. Your canvas boat bag is perfect for holding everything you need to take to a shower. With its handles and waterproof base it can be looped onto a hook in the shower or set onto a damp floor without getting what's inside wet. When outfitting your crew, give everyone a pair of inexpensive rubber pharmacy thongs to wear to, during, and from the shower in warm weather. They will keep feet sanitary, despite shower floor conditions, and reduce the risk of contracting athlete's foot. If it is too cool to walk outdoors with nearly bare feet, pack the thongs in the shower tote along with other supplies. If you can, though, limit the contents of your tote to the essential shampoo, soap, and towel. The fewer items you have to fiddle with, the sooner you can be out of the shower stall and allow the next person in line to get clean.

Men seem to be able to get in and out of a shower more quickly than women do, probably because they don't shave their legs or fuss with hair conditioners and skin moisturizers. Additional items that most women require for complete grooming are a razor, deodorant, talcum, hair conditioner, toothbrush, toothpaste, hairbrush, hair dryer, and a full set of makeup. Hanging cosmetic bags work well to organize and contain these small items; the ones with removable inserts that can be hung on the showerhead are an especially good choice. Organize your tote so you can get at the things you'll need in order of their use. After all, you may be delving into that tote hanging from one hook and have nowhere but a wet shelf to set anything down.

This is how I do it. I set up the stall when I first enter it by hanging up my towel so I can grab it and wrap it around me as soon as I emerge in my wet glory. I use a thin, cotton bath sheet for maximum coverage. Not all showers have privacy curtains and I no longer have a body I wish to flaunt. Next, I remove my soap, shampoo, and anything else I will use in the shower and set them either inside the shower or just outside the stall on a shelf or the floor. I wear my rubber thongs throughout my shower.

HE SAID: *"Are you going swimming?"*
SHE SAID: *"No, I'm on my way to the shower."*

In warm weather, I find that a bathing suit makes perfect shower attire. I wear my suit to the shower, using my towel or an old T-shirt as a cover-up. I remove my suit to bathe, rinsing it out at the same time, and either put on a fresh dry suit, or climb back into my clean, cold, wet one. I often wait to make up my face, dry my hair, and put on fresh clothes until I reach the comfort of my own boat. That way, my clothes are less likely to get wet or dirty before I've had a chance to wear them. I just swaddle the towel around my head, turban style, put on my sunglasses, and slither back to our boat hoping no one will recognize me.

The busiest showering hours at marinas are between eight and nine o'clock in the morning and four and six o'clock in the afternoon. Luxuriating in long showers, as if you were at home, is a thoughtless thing to do during those busy times. The hot water disappears quickly and all those nice people patiently waiting in line behind you get a cold shower. Before you leave your shower stall, check to be sure you have all your gear with you. No one wants to deal with discarded soap wrappers and empty shampoo bottles.

SHOWERLESS?

If you are on a trip and shore showers are unavailable, you may be forced to resort to alternate ways to get that salt off your skin before bedtime. If your boat doesn't have a shower, it probably doesn't have hot water either. But you don't have to live with discomfort. In cool weather, you can always take a sponge bath using water you've warmed to tepid in a pot on the stove. Even if you are stuck using cold water, the simple act of wiping down your skin with a wet, lightly soaped washcloth will make you feel clean and refreshed. In warm weather, and in clean anchorages, take a sea bath, remembering to use soap and shampoo that lather in salt water. Rinse off with fresh water from a bottle or with water from a solar water bag that's been heated by the sun.

Solar water bags, which can be purchased at marine stores or through catalogs, work nicely for those of us who don't have built-in showers on their boats, or who wish to conserve their boat's water. (If you haven't seen one before, they look similar to an old-fashioned enema bag, but of course are used quite differently.) Fill the bag ashore and secure it topside while under way. Unless it's a freezing cold and dreary day, you'll soon have enough warm water for a quick shower or two. If it's warm enough for an outdoor shower, hang the solar bag from the mast or boom. You can even buy a shower curtain to go with these bags.

You can also use a solar water bag in the privacy of your head in cool weather, or in the evening after the sun has gone down. Simply erect the bag in the head from a high hook. If this won't work for you, try mounting the bag outdoors near the head's hatch or porthole, and then snake the spray nozzle through the opening. One comment about water bag showers—the water kind of dribbles from the nozzle because there is so little water pressure. Use shampoo and soap sparingly because it may not rinse off easily. I've read that there are gadgets you can buy to increase the water pressure on these bags. If solar bags are going to be your primary means of showering, they might be worth the expense.

SHOWERING ON A BOAT

Most built-in boat showers are akin to using the spray on a kitchen sink. They normally consist of a narrow hose with a spray nozzle, an off/on switch, and an erratic temperature control. Unless you have a pressurized water system, you will probably have to use a foot or hand pump to bring water through the showerhead. On many boats, the entire head is the shower area, so everything gets wet. Depending on the layout of your head, it may be possible to mount a plastic curtain that will protect the toilet and sink area and keep them dry.

Not all boats have a hot-water tank. Our first one didn't, but we had a shower. A wonderful, cold-water shower we never used. There are so few times during a summer in the Northeast that a cold shower is welcome.

Even when we bought our next boat, which had hot and cold pressurized water, it took us a while to get comfortable using the shower. We were finally motivated to use it when we attended a regatta. All the marina could offer our 60 boats was two plank-floored shower stalls, each equipped with a single shower nozzle and a clothes hook. The weather was torrid and we worked up a sweat just imagining fighting the shower line. That weekend, we learned to enjoy the privacy and convenience of showering on our own boat. I styled my hair for the first time without a hair dryer and used the extra time to make a batch of piña coladas in our 12-volt blender.

The average boater with a perfectly adequate onboard shower will often use it only as a last resort. Empty space in the head tends to be a catchall for wet gear, laundry bags, duffel storage, ice chests, and anything else that's bulky to stow. So, it seems a chore to clear it away to take a shower. If this is your problem, resolve it by grouping the contents of your shower in easily removable chunks. Stuff all the empty duffels into one large one so you can remove them all with one grab. Use hangers for gear or clothes so you can rehang them elsewhere while you shower.

If you keep your shower area clean, mildew free, and ready to use, you, too, may find yourself hooked on the privacy and comfort of showering on your boat. One caution though—be sure the bilge pump is on and ready to drain when you shower or you'll be walking on water. Not all bilge pumps are automatic. I'll never forget the day I was merrily showering in our head when I noticed that the bath mat was floating. I cracked open the door to a mess. The water drained out as soon as I switched on the bilge pump, but the rug and all the stuff sitting on the sole didn't dry for days.

To conserve the water in your tanks, keep boat showers short and functional. Rinse, shut off the water and soap up, then final rinse. Perform extraneous tasks you might do in your shower at home, such as brushing your teeth and shaving your legs, in the same manner, or do them elsewhere. You can further trim your shower time with dual-function products like leave-in hair conditioners, soap and moisturizer combinations, and shampoos that double as body washes.

For me, luxury is having an outdoor shower hose in the cockpit. These are sometimes equipped with the same temperature control as the inside shower, and are terrific for rinsing off salt water after a swim and keeping the shower mess out of your boat. Just remember that cockpit showers draw on the fresh water tanks, so don't get carried away.

If you are on an extended trip, water consumption can become a real issue. Knowing the capacity of your water tanks and how often you need to refill them will help you plan your stops. This is especially important if you've got several people showering aboard. Guests are water hogs. You'll likely run out of hot water before the last person has showered. (You'll know this is the case when a piercing yelp emits from the head.) To keep water hot throughout a series of showers, try running the engine to keep the hot water supply coming.

CHAPTER

21

Home Is Where You Drop Your Anchor

WHERE TO LIVE?

When your boat is at rest, so are you. No matter whether you're docked at your home port or at a vacation spot, the water becomes your womb, encasing your boat in the delicious sounds and feel of flotation. You'll sleep like a baby and eat like a mad person. Dockage comes in three delicious flavors: a mooring, an anchorage, or a slip. Being on a mooring or at anchor is comparable to living in a house because you can make noise and have some degree of privacy without worrying about disturbing your neighbors. Being at a slip is like being in an apartment—your neighbors know all. Moorings, anchorages, and slips each have their own set of merits and inconveniences. I've enjoyed them all and, although I'm a "dock dolly" now, I'll always cherish special mooring moments.

MORE ABOUT MOORINGS AND ANCHORAGES

As you give yourself over to the silent caress of water against your hull, you'll languish in almost total seclusion—until the giggles of a dinghy full of people riding by shock you back to reality. The wind traps and dulls distant sounds around you and you forget how close you are to land until a siren or honk of a car horn interrupts the water-oriented sounds you've come to accept as normal.

Time Alone

For the active person who deals with people all week, a mooring or anchorage can be a restorative haven. You can choose to be alone. There are no passersby to peer into your hatches and through your portholes, or to stop by to chat. Yet, the bustle of shore life is just a short dinghy ride away any time you wish it. You don't even have to worry about socializing with boaters moored nearby. Unless the wind is blowing in the right direction, you won't be able to hold a conversation with them. All you have to do is wave and smile.

Blast your tunes or have an orgy and no one will care. Of course, if it sounds like you're having a good time, your neighbors may come over in their dinghy to join you. We've had some of our best parties on a mooring. When our boat got too loaded to hold any more people, we just sent the overflow to their dinghies. What's nice about this arrangement is that, when you've had it with the crowds, you can just cut their dinghies loose and go to bed!

A Constant Breeze

On a mooring or at anchor, your bow will always point to the wind (unless some really strong current is playing games with the wind), making conditions on your boat somewhat predictable. On scorching summer days, this is the place to be. You'll pick up any breeze that's out there as you rotate around a mooring buoy or anchor—and the mosquitoes will be so busy plaguing the people on the docks they won't be interested in making the journey out to bother you. As your boat lazily makes its 360° circle, you'll relax in the gentle sense of movement and enjoy an interesting panoramic view of the neighborhood.

You know that it will always be cooler on the bow than in the cockpit because the bow catches the first breeze. If you have a dodger or canopy over your companionway, it will block the wind on a cool day and allow you to enjoy the warmth of the sun. We found that barbecuing off the stern at a mooring is ideal because the wind blows the flames and fumes away from the boat, not into it.

"Comfort" in a Blow

A boat on a mooring or at anchor has more freedom of movement. Thus, it can float with a wave or undulate with a gust of wind. This same boat docked in a slip, however, would be fighting dock restraints. In turbulent conditions, a boat on a mooring or at anchor is often more comfortable because there is no dock to bang up against and restraining docklines to fight.

Of course, the reliability of being at anchor under adverse conditions is only as good as the expertise and foresight of the captain. When high winds and heavy seas are forecast, make certain you are in a protected harbor that is away from, or in the lee of, the dominant wind direction. If anchoring, choose good holding ground. Even a well-set anchor can pull loose with tidal changes, so it must be checked frequently.

Some style of anchors hold better in certain conditions than others, but any anchor must be large enough to hold your boat in a variety of circumstances. If you are not adept at anchoring, invest in an anchor alarm to signal you if the anchor pulls loose. It took us a long time before we could sleep comfortably at anchor. We had numerous fire drills, which always seemed to occur in the middle of the night. When our anchor pulled loose, we awakened to the sound of our boat thumping into a nearby boat. Take my advice and don't sleep naked when you are at anchor, because it's important to move fast if things go awry.

The Safety of Moorings

Moorings offer more stability than anchors because a mooring block—the part of the mooring that's buried on the ocean's floor—isn't going to go anywhere under most conditions. Whatever the block consists of—a heavy mushroom anchor, an enormous chunk of concrete, or some other seriously heavy object—it's virtually impossible to pull it loose once it digs in and immerses itself. The only danger that moorings present in heavy weather is if the mooring line is frayed or too small. The violent up-and-down motion of a moored boat in a storm can easily chafe the line and set your boat free to romp through the mooring field.

Be certain that the mooring you select is the correct size for your boat. For example, a 15-foot boat requires a less substantial mooring buoy than a 45-foot boat. However, most mooring markers look the same. If your boat is large, and this important information is not indicated on the mooring buoy, seek the dockmaster. He or she can often suggest the right mooring for you. Once you've moored, check that the line you've picked up is sized in proportion to your boat and that it is not frayed. You may need to reinforce it by looping a line of your own through as well. Now you can relax. Your boat is unlikely to pull off the mooring, even in hurricane-force winds—although do not by choice ride out a storm at a mooring. Once the boat is secure, get off it and run for cover.

Getting Ashore

Nothing's perfect though, is it? Moorings and anchorages are wonderful—until you need to go ashore in foul weather. Shrouded in your woolies, you descend into the dinghy and are reminded as soon as you sit down that you should have worn your foul-weather pants, or at least brought something dry to sit on. You'll arrive ashore a little soggy and bedraggled, but that's a small price to pay for privacy and contentment. Like everything else in boating, you soon figure out how to make the best of any situation.

MORE ABOUT DOCKS

It's a toss-up. As much as I love the tranquillity of a mooring or an anchorage, it's hard to beat the convenience and buzz of activity at a dock. Being hooked into dockside power means you can use your electrical appliances with (almost) gay abandon. I say almost because you can easily get carried away and run too many appliances at once and blow a fuse.

When we went back to a slip after many years on a mooring, one of our first problems was learning how to barbecue at a dock. On our mooring, we were never concerned about wind direction while barbecuing because we were always pointed into the wind. This is definitely not the case at a dock. Wind can be blowing over your boat from any direction—not just from the bow. The first time we tried to cook steaks on the grill at dock, the wind was blowing right into our cockpit. We were afraid to chance lighting the coals because of the fire hazard, so I seared our steaks in a skillet that night. Like all new experiences, we just needed to think things through. We looked around and noticed that our neighbors had placed their grills on the pier in the lee of the wind. Our ball-shaped little kettle wouldn't sit flat on the pier, so we investigated further and bought a detachable stand for it, which solved our problem.

Moving our grill to the pier meant that we moved the focus of our evening activity from our cockpit. The men began socializing and it wasn't long before a few lawn chairs, shade umbrellas, and a small table for snacks were in place. One neighbor even rigged up a pipe with a showerhead onto his hose and offered us all a place to take a cold shower after a swim. Next year, he's adding a curtain.

SHE SAID: *"My hairdryer just stopped working."*

HE SAID: *"Well, what other things are you running?"*

SHE SAID: *"I'm microwaving your oatmeal and making your toast."*

Summer at "H" Dock

At almost any time of day, particularly in nonboating weather, a varying combination of neighbors share our dock seats. Some for a few minutes, some for hours. Occasionally we drag out our blenders and have blender wars, sampling and judging who can make the best mudslide or piña colada. Plates of chips and snacks appear and, as dinnertime approaches, we fire up our grills and share our meals, or pair off and head out to a restaurant. Our dock has earned the dubious reputation of being the party dock at our marina.

At the end of the evening, the brilliance of the stars or a full, red moon brings us out of our cockpits and onto the pier, where we pass around binoculars and point out star groups. One chilly evening, we even dragged the space heater off one of our boats and plugged it into shoreside power to keep our feet warm. Before long, someone handed out cigars and brought out a bottle of fine port and a few glasses. Our gentle chatter continued until the last person yawned and drifted off to his berth.

Moving to the high society of a dock after the restorative peacefulness of a mooring was a big adjustment for me. I must have appeared a recluse for the first year because I steered clear of the circle of chairs on the dock, preferring the haven of my own quiet cockpit. It took me most of that first season to reconcile my feelings and mentally adjust to the change. Everything seemed too easy. Each time I abandoned my cockpit to join the gang on the

pier, I felt like I was leaving a dear friend alone. My husband was quite unhappy with my antisocial behavior. He, in the meantime, had become a Jolly Roger and was thriving on the extra opportunities to talk about our boat.

Then I finally saw the light. I could step directly off my boat onto dry land without getting into a dinghy. I didn't have to conserve the water in our tanks because more was a mere hose and faucet away. I liked being able to easily walk up to the marina's head to use its facilities instead of ours. I noticed that our boat stayed clean because the bulk of the entertaining had moved onto the pier. Also, we'd made many wonderful new friends. I found that whenever I tired of all the fuss on the dock, I could simply retire to our boat. I could take a nap, read in the cockpit, or visit privately with a friend.

Our dock neighbors have always been considerate, and I believe this is typical among boaters. As a rule, we respect each other's privacy. We don't hop aboard without an invitation anymore than we would enter a home without knocking. So I found I still had my peace and tranquility; it had always been there waiting for me on my boat. But when I'm in the mood to gab or take a walk, I can simply step onto the dock and do it. My boat will always be my home on the water, but I've decided that the dock makes a great backyard.

I love being on a dock for several reasons: I don't have to hassle with getting in and out of the dinghy; our marine head doesn't need to be pumped out as often because it's less used (we almost always opt to use the marina's head); and it's nice to walk into a restaurant wearing dry clothes. We still enjoy anchoring when we're sailing, but doing so seems like camping now. We thoroughly enjoy coming home to our slip, our dock, where we shamelessly enjoy all the comforts of home.

Dock Drawbacks

WATER, WATER, EVERYWHERE Water! There's too much of it on a dock! No longer do we have an excuse not to keep our boats clean. Dockers are hosers. A hose must be an extension of the male ego that entices them to keep it up and running, ready to rinse, suds, or whatever at the slightest spec of dust or salt. I must admit, though, it is nice to be able to use all the water we want on our boat with a refill just a hose away.

NOT ENOUGH MOTION Your boat will hold pretty steady when it is in its slip unless the slip is in a thoroughfare, channel, or frequented path. Most marinas have a no-wake law that prohibits boats from exceeding 5 mph. In fact, you may even forget you are on a boat until the jolt of a wake brings you back. If a storm comes up—well that's different.

TOO MUCH MOTION A dock may not be the best place to be in a storm. A restrained boat is an unhappy one when bucking heavy winds and angry seas. In a slip, you're surrounded by lots of dock to clank against as waves lift your boat up and down and from side to side. It will be noisy as the wind whistles through the rigging, and you'll be kept awake at night listening to much more noise than you'll ever hear at anchor. But still, it's a small price to pay for all the luxuries of being at a dock.

If a storm is brewing you should take several precautions to protect your boat. At the end of one particularly ferocious summer we were hit with hurricane warnings on three consecutive weekends. Each weekend we did this drill: We removed all of our topside canvas, including the dodger and bimini, and secured anything else that could possible flap. We reinforced all of our docklines, tied extra lines around our masts, and removed all detachable, external gear, such as our barbecue grill, that were liable to break loose and go flying.

We anticipated 65 mph winds at our exposed, outside slip, so our marina assigned us a more protected one. One weekend we joined our boating buddies, who also had remained at the marina to watch their babies, and had a hurricane party. We were interviewed and filmed for the local evening news as we barbecued steaks. Many of us spent a sleepless night aboard rocking and rolling, and waiting for the storm to hit. Some folks got paranoid and moved to their cars to get some rest. Me? I drove home.

If you expect bad weather, keep in mind that you have options. You can always take your boat out to a mooring, preferably one on the lee side of the storm, if you want to get away from a slip. All of the major sailing magazines regularly print excellent articles on how to prepare a boat for a storm. Read them!

COSTLY CONVENIENCES After a while, cost becomes irrelevant in boating. Everything costs more than we care to pay. Yes, a slip is more expensive than a mooring. Anchorages are the only facilities left that are free. But with a slip, you get what you pay for—electricity, water, and many of the comforts of home.

GOING ASHORE?

When leaving your boat, even for a few hours, it's always smart to shut the hatches and portholes unless you're positive it won't rain. A few other things to consider: If you are taking the dinghy out, can you find you way back in the dark or the fog? Should you lock your boat? If at a dock, are your lines secure? If at anchor, are you sure your anchor is holding? If the tides or wind direction change, how will that affect your boat? Take a few minutes to think, then go have a good time.

Should You Lock Up?

"Just for a few hours," we think as we head out. Many boaters don't even think about locking their boats. We leave them, with all our belongings and expensive electronic gear, open and unattended. We may close the companionway to deter entry, but most of us would probably admit that we don't bother to lock up.

Why is this, I wonder? We wouldn't think of leaving our car unlocked in a public lot, and we go to great lengths to use deadbolts and other burglarproof devices in our homes. Yet we rely on a wimpy padlock to secure our boat—a boat which, in some instances, may be worth more than our houses. Perhaps we think of the marina as our home and feel that our boat will be secure amongst other boaters, our family.

The reality is that the average marina provides little or no security to mariners. They guard their restrooms more dutifully than they protect the boats in their yards. A visitor may need to ask for a key to use the restroom, but is free to stroll the docks. An unlocked gate and a warning sign will not keep serious prowlers out. Marinas that are situated in highly populated tourist areas, or with popular restaurants on site, are most susceptible to security problems.

In our 20 years of sailing, the only near invasion we had was two summers ago when cruising the Cape Cod area. After a wonderful meal at a marina's on-premise restaurant, we were slumbering in our berths when we awoke with a start to the sounds of people boarding our boat. Perhaps they just wanted to sit on it and look at the moon. Whatever their reason, they sure ran when my husband called out to them. Thereafter, we installed an interior sliding lock on our companionway hatch so now we can sleep securely and worry-free at strange marinas.

At our home port though, we tend to leave our boat open, especially if many of our friends are out and about, and we have never had a problem. Our neighbors would certainly be suspicious of a stranger boarding our boat. On vacation, however, we always lock the boat when we are not on it. Sometimes we leave a lower hatchboard out to allow for ventilation, but not entry. My advice is that, if you have any doubts about security, lock your boat.

Dinghying 101

I highly recommend that you learn how to operate your dinghy, whether that entails learning how to row or operate an outboard engine. Get adept at pulling a start cord to start the engine, maneuvering the tiller, and controlling the speed. Think of a dinghy as your freedom. Being abandoned on a mooring or at an anchorage without transportation to shore, or to someone else's boat, is like being at home without a car.

If you don't know how to operate your dinghy, you will be obligated to depend on someone else to haul you about, at his or her convenience. Ask me, I know. I don't do dinghies. (I also don't pump my own gas.) It's a rebellion thing. Oh, I can operate our dinghy in an emergency, but most of the time I enjoy playing the helpless female and taking advantage of a free ride with a handsome chauffeur. But I'm probably from a different era than you are, so don't go by my example. I see small children operating dinghies. Certainly you can.

Finding Your Boat in the Dark

Returning to your boat after an evening ashore will not be a problem if your boat is at a slip, unless you've had too much to drink. If you are on a mooring or at anchor, however, you will either ride on a marina-provided launch or use your dinghy. Often, it's the dinghy. Whenever you leave your boat and do not plan to return until after dark, leave a light on inside to make identification easier upon your return. Some boaters use colored light bulbs to distinguish their boat from all the others in the anchorage. Placing a red lens over a cabin light—usually a chart table light—is a common practice on boats because the color red is easier on the eyes when going from a light to dark (or vice versa) environment. Therefore, a lamp with a red lens is a particularly good night-light. A lit interior will also allow you to enter your boat in the dark without tripping over the steps.

If you are using your dinghy to go ashore, mark your way by paying attention to landmarks, nearby boat names, and other identifying markers you encounter as you head into shore. At night, travel with a handheld compass and flashlight in your dinghy. Note your course going to shore and then add 180° to get your return course. This simple procedure can get you home some evening when the fog rolls in.

It's a bad idea to leave anything you value in plain view in a dinghy when it is secured to a dock because some people like to borrow gear from dinghies. We've had life jackets stolen, and people have borrowed our oars, taken our flashlight, and even used our dinghy. If you are in a questionable area for security—lock it up.

AND TOTES, TOO! Unless your dinghy is elaborate enough to have enclosed storage areas, you will likely be lugging your belongings with you onto shore. Seasoned boaters find that a large waterproof boat bag works fine for this purpose. If you are returning to your boat in the evening, you can expect that it will often be covered with moisture. Stow a towel in your tote to sit on or to wipe down the seating areas, and take along extra windbreakers or sweatshirts for the chilly ride back.

Looking Good When You Land

One of the most frustrating things we women have to deal with when boating is expending the effort to get all dressed up, only to have our makeup and hair ruined on the ride into shore. For those times when you care about arriving ashore looking presentable, try these tricks passed on to me by a good friend who's learned how to beat the odds.

- ○ Wear your foul-weather jacket or a lightweight, waterproof, hooded windjacket and pull the hood lightly over your hair. The longer the jacket, the drier your clothes will remain.
- ○ Wear a clip-on visor to keep the jacket hood from flopping onto your forehead and crushing your coiffure, and to protect your face from the wind.
- ○ Put on your glasses or sunglasses to keep the wind from making your eyes tear, thus ruining your eye makeup.
- ○ Huddle at the rear of the boat (how wet you get is proportionate to how far forward you sit) and keep your head down, gripping the base of your hood so it doesn't blow off.
- ○ As you slow down going into the dock, remove the hood, and fluff up your hair.
- ○ Once tied up, put the jacket and the visor into your shore tote; make your husband carry it.

○ If it's warm, get into the dinghy barefoot; if not, wear your
boat shoes for the ride ashore. Slip on your pretty sandals once you dock.

Voilà! You're gorgeous! Your hair, makeup, clothing, and sandals look fresh and pretty, just as if you stepped out of a car.

Dining Out

Cruising guides, local tourist information centers, and word-of-
mouth recommendations are good sources of information for dining out. Collect matchbooks from the places you like the best, or
record them in your journal, so you will remember which ones to
revisit. When we dine out, we want to enjoy the best restaurants in

the area (after all, we're on vacation), but we've learned that we can get away with leaving our dressy clothes at home. Sport jackets, ties, linen dresses, and pumps are not boat friendly—they're a nuisance to store as well as to keep looking fresh and crisp.

It can be awkward getting on and off your boat or riding a dinghy into shore if you have clothes that will be damaged by water, or may get in the way. For the summertime, there are so many choices. In my experience, I've found that a sundress and a pair of sandals can go almost anywhere. Dress your outfit up or down with change of jewelry. For men, chino slacks and a collared polo shirt are acceptable in all but the stuffiest of restaurants. Most shoreline restaurants are pretty tolerant of the boating crowd they attract and will forgive almost any attire as long as it's clean and neat. If your restaurant of choice won't accept you as you are dressed, ask if they serve in the bar. You'll still enjoy the ambiance, although with a somewhat rowdier crowd.

CHAPTER

22

It's All in Fun

THE POSSIBILITIES ARE ENDLESS

Boating is fun, so lighten up on the serious stuff whenever you can. The only thing better than a boat under sail is a boat at ease. Take advantage of a rainy afternoon to enjoy simple pleasures. Do a watercolor, write poetry, or read a trashy novel. Get out the binoculars and scan the horizon: watch a regatta or peer into the backyards of fabulous seaside estates. Snap some photos to blow up to poster size and tack on the walls of your office. Play your favorite music. Get a party going. Fun is waiting for you, so do it. Have fun!

SOCIALIZE

It must be the salt air that makes boaters so friendly. And how can one not be relaxed? Boating squeezes stress right out of our bodies. It's no wonder our boating friends think we are always placid and easygoing—they haven't seen our work personas. No one knows what a tough week we've had because our other lives seem so remote when we are on our boats that we don't even think to discuss them.

Picture a marina or anchorage full of people who fit this description and you've got the makings for a great party and some nice friendships. People wave and say hello. They stop by your boat to chat. The kids get acquainted and they're off doing healthy things like fishing, crabbing, or looking for shells. If a boat is coming into a slip, folks go out of their way to catch the lines. If they see that another boat is having a problem, they all hurry to assist. We're never alone when caring people surround us.

In the boating environment, people drop their barriers and become human. The woman behind me in the shower line is liable to be the CEO of a large company, but I'll probably never know because the subject rarely comes up. All she and I will talk about are mundane things like the weather, where we sailed today, and which ports have the best restaurants and shopping. We may even share shampoo across the shower, or hand off some toilet paper under the stall. We'll continue our talk later when we drop by each other's boats for a cocktail and a tour. That is how boating friendships are. Our work world identity disappears and we become the nice people we were intended to be.

WATER SPORTS

Summertime and water are a natural combination. When we're relaxing, or perhaps a bit bored, there are always some enjoyable things we can do to please ourselves and stir up some fun with our fellow boaters.

Wash the Boat

Stroll along the docks on any nice day and I guarantee you'll see at least two or three boaters, maybe more, cleaning their boats. Boats are like beautiful pieces of expensive jewelry that we want to keep shiny and looking new so we can show them off. Everything must be just so. The stainless steel stanchions must be polished, the fiberglass buffed, and the brightwork sanded and varnished. We should keep our houses in as good shape as our boats. In rainy weather, we sometimes put on our foul-weather gear and soap up the boat—it's something to do besides huddling belowdecks with a good book, taking a nap, or finding a local bar (although we sometimes do all that stuff afterwards). Cleaning boats at a marina is a social activity. It's a good excuse to exchange tips and borrow hoses and interact with fellow boaters.

Pick a Fight

A spray of water can be invigorating on a blistering hot day, so do it. Start a water fight. The choices of artillery are endless. If you have children you probably have at least one long-distance water pistol. Drag it out and set your aim for your neighbor who's taking a snooze in the cockpit. Retaliation will be quick and you're on your way. Get in the dinghy and stir up some more trouble. Soon, you won't be alone. Your friends will be chasing you with buckets of water and you'll love it.

Are water balloons still legal? We had some crazy times launching them a few years back, before biodegradable became a household word. One enthusiastic friend using a balloon launcher had his face in the way when the balloon ricocheted—and splat! So, we resorted to alternative methods. We refined our craft. We used balloons that were specifically designed for water fights because they burst on impact, which is important because unbroken balloons get lobbed back at you. We divided into two teams, the loaders and the tossers. As leader of the team in charge of filling the balloons, I found that the neck of a balloon fits nicely over the skinny faucet on our saltwater pump, so no need to waste fresh water. Sometimes, though, our targets got more than a salt-water shower. Our salt-water pump was toggled to the ice chest water drain and every once in a while, I forgot to switch it over.

If you want to start a water fight, load up your crew with a bucket of filled balloons. If you don't want to use balloons, provide them with buckets full of water and some paper cups, or a long-distance water pistol, and send them off in the dinghy. This strategy moves the fight off your boat while wetting down the cockpits of those around you. Before you know it, everyone will be out motoring in their dinghies, tossing water at each other, using any containers they have on hand. The adults have the most fun. No question.

Play with Water Toys

Go to any toy or sporting goods store, or to a chandlery, and look around—you'll find all kinds of water toys and flotation devices. The ocean's your swimming pool. Pull the kids along in a giant tube behind your dinghy, or float atop a queen-sized raft with a friend. Tether your flotation device to your boat, and you won't go adrift. Jump in the water with a floating cushion or life preserver and paddle effortlessly around your boat. Sit on it when you get tired. Even if you don't swim, like me, you can still enjoy the water.

I snorkel with a life preserver on. Just wrap yourself up in a PFD and dive in.

ENTERTAIN YOURSELVES ON BOARD

If you've got fleas in your shorts and are tired of relaxing, there's plenty around you to think about and do without harassing any of your neighbors.

Take Pictures

I always keep a camera handy on board so I can catch a great shot—although I am often disappointed when I get my pictures back because my camera never seems to capture the beauty that I see through its lens: the spark of the sun against a white hull, the vibrant colors of flying spinnakers, the energy of a tack, the salty smell of waves crashing high against a lighthouse. At first I thought there was something wrong with my camera, so we bought a new one with ranges for distance and close-up shots. Didn't help. Maybe I'm just a lousy photographer, but no matter how hard I try, a flat picture never duplicates what I feel when I'm on the water.

Flip through Sailing Magazines

Most boaters own a library's worth of nautical books and magazines. Some are instructional, some are informative, some are humorous. The most fun book we own is a how-to manual on knot making, which comes with bright red-and-blue shoelaces to practice with. This book will keep a restless adolescent fascinated for hours, but I'll be darned if I can get some of those knots tied right. There are enough boating magazines and newsletters published today to fill a container ship. An avid reader can be kept busy for months. I avoid those that are too technical or nonapplicable to the tasks I need to deal with—I fall asleep just flipping through those pages, while my husband thrives on them. It doesn't take long for anyone who's new to boating to acquire a good-sized collection of onboard reading material.

Make Knots

If you haven't learned to make nautical knots yet, get some nylon cord and a good book on the subject, and try. If you've ever done macramé, nautical knots should be a snap for you to figure out. Learn the functional knots first; if you enjoy doing those, go on to the decorative knots. A good buddy of mine always attracts crowds when he laces up a Turk's head knot on a steering wheel. The knot is a circular, continuously laced band with seemingly no beginning and no end; it is knotted at the center point on a ship's wheel. It also can be worn decoratively around an ankle or wrist—but it has to be cut off to be removed, which you will want to do when it gets dirty.

Read Books

We always keep a supply of instructional boating books aboard for reference—see the reference list in the appendix for recommendations. In addition to our nautical reading supply, I keep some good novels. In the summer I normally opt for light, fluffy stuff; my captain thrives on war books and murder mysteries. I leave novels that I've enjoyed on board so I can barter with a friend for something I haven't read yet. Our marina has a book exchange where I can pick up new reading material in trade for the book I've just completed.

Listen to Music—the Soul of Sailing

What better way is there to celebrate being on the water than with music? It's so easy to enjoy your favorite tunes. Bring a portable radio, cassette, or CD player to your boat and set it in a snug spot on a small piece of rubber so it won't bounce around.

For thousands of sailors, Jimmy Buffet's songs symbolize the boating lifestyle. His relaxed and happy music evokes images of hot Caribbean sands and clear turquoise waters. My captain and I enjoy listening to instrumental music on invigorating sails— themes from movies like *Dances with Wolves* and *The Last of the Mohicans*. We save listening to the *Titanic* CD for when we are safely into port, though. When we get droopy, we blast the scores from

Top Gun or *Good Morning Vietnam*. New-age music from Yanni, George Winston, and Jim Brickman enhance the beauty of a sunset or a starlit night.

Collect Boat Names

The names that people give their boats never cease to amaze me. It's great fun to try to imagine how a boat got its name. Almost always, a name tells you something about the owner. The visual picture I get from *Irma's Mink* is of a woman (named Irma!) wearing a cloth coat while her husband is dressed in a big sappy smile. You have to wonder about a guy, and it has to be a guy, who names his boat *Foreplay*. Or how about *Ship of Fools?* Some people incorporate their own names into their boats' names, such as *Fidler on the Sea*, *Mac Attack*, or *Sea Bob*. Some can't escape their careers: *White Tooth* (a dentist) or *Blue Data* (a computer specialist).

Boat names are sometimes a clever combination of family names, such as *Ron-Di-Vous* (Ron, Diane, and—I guess—you), or express action, such as *Go For It* or *Impulse*. Our first boat was named after our deceased dog, *Mitzi-ann*. I'm sure people thought she was my husband's mistress. I lobbied for a name change and, henceforth, our next boat was named *Joy of Summer*. Our present boat is called *Joy For All Seasons* because we use it year-round.

Watch Other Boaters Make Mistakes

We find it's great cocktail hour entertainment to watch the contortions that boaters go through to set anchor or pick up a mooring. Yes, I know it's not nice to laugh at other people's expense—but their antics can be so funny. Boating novices often can't appreciate this somewhat perverse sense of humor, but they will eventually.

We recently watched in disbelief as a sailboat attempting to set anchor motored thoughtlessly over a small powerboat's anchor rode and set it afloat. We contacted the harbormaster to help rectify the situation because the owner of the small powerboat was not on board. If your anchor rode is cut when you are on board, you will know it. The movement on your boat will suddenly change and you will feel a slight jerk and possibly a thump. That will be your boat colliding with another. If this happens to you, quickly get the engine going, get your boat under control, and reset a second anchor—you *do* carry a second anchor, don't you?

Another boating couple, deciding to sail out of the harbor, forgot to free their mooring ball. We laughed hysterically as they dragged the ball in circles around the harbor. Some kind soul finally dinghied out to let the captain know why they weren't progressing. Our entertainment often consists of watching people making several attempts to pick up a mooring ball with their boathook. We're not mean, though. We've taken our dinghy over to help out many times. After all, every one of us has at some point experienced the embarrassment of missing the mark. We all try to look like we know what we are doing, but with errant wind conditions, changing currents, and tidal constraints, trying to anchor, pick up a mooring, or dock smoothly is always a turkey shoot.

My captain loves to stand in our cockpit and play traffic cop, shaking his fist and shouting obscenities at boaters violating the "no wake" rule—a 5-mph speed limit is imposed in almost every anchorage or marina on the East Coast. I don't know how he expects the offenders can hear him over the roar of their engines, let alone take heed.

Blow Bubbles

Stow a bottle of children's bubbles aboard and you can amuse yourself and those around you while enjoying a leisurely sail. Blow bubbles when you are sailing into the wind and they will stream out in your wake. They take on a phosphorescence in the sun and look fantastic.

Take a Spinnaker Ride

I saw this done in the British Virgin Islands, and judging from the screams I heard, it must be lots of fun. If you are the type who likes parasailing and bungee jumping, this may be your sea bag. The bo'sun's chair is tied to the spinnaker line, and the joy rider sits on the chair. When the spinnaker is released, the rider flies high. The smart person, who chooses not to take a turn, controls the lines for the spinnaker from the cockpit. This is not for the inexperienced or chicken hearted.

Cruise with a Flotilla

Forming a flotilla with friends can make a great trip magnificent. Agree on a radio channel to monitor and maintain contact throughout your trip. This way, all the boats benefit from the expertise and sophistication of the navigational tools of the lead boater. There's safety in numbers. If it is foggy, a lead boat with radar can help you navigate through the haze. Should your engine fail or you go aground, it's comforting to know that a fellow boater is nearby to assist you. Each summer we make passage to Cape Cod in a flock of four to six boats. We stop at many of the same harbors and usually get together in the evening for cocktails or dinner. We gather for lazy days on the beach, sip cold drinks, and watch our kids have a grand time in the water. We break off in groups to go shopping or to explore our stopping ports. If it's rainy or foggy, we may sit inside our own boats and read or nap, or buzz around in our dinghies swathed in foul-weather gear, invading each other's boats and begging cold beers.

BOAT SHOWS

Boat shows help us seasonal sailors survive the winter, and they afford a wonderful opportunity to talk with the dealers and manufacturers of boats and boating-related products. Every boating magazine on the market lists the shows' schedules; on the East Coast, they usually run from early fall through spring. Whatever your preference—power, sail, small boats, big boats, wooden boats, used boats—you'll find a show to pique your interest. If you are considering buying your first boat or upgrading to a bigger one, this is the best time to collect information.

You'll especially enjoy the in-the-water shows where you can tour outrageously expensive boats that you would normally not have an opportunity to set foot on. Some of these yachts cost upwards of two million dollars and attract crowds, so get there early. The lines get longer as the day wears on. And by the way— no matter how badly you have to use the bathroom, *never* use the heads on show boats. Find out where the restrooms are and get in line.

New boats that are ordered in the fall are built over the winter for spring delivery, so you can usually get exactly what you want for a good price. However, if you purchase a boat in the fall, you will have the devil of a time getting your captain through the winter. He'll fall asleep each night with the boat's brochure tucked under his pillow. "New boat" winters are the longest ones, but you'll be rewarded in the spring when your brand-new boat is delivered, pristine clean and bottom painted. Even if you aren't in the market for a new boat, go to a show and find out what's new. Just walking on a boat off-season will send chills up your spine and evoke visions of summer.

Chances are that you'll run into boating buddies at one of these shows. Maybe you can help them spend their money instead of you spending yours. Oh, did I mention that boat shows are expensive? Even if you aren't in the market for a new boat, you'll find every gadget in the world at a boat show. No matter how many shows we attend, and we hardly miss a one, we can always find something new we didn't know we needed. I usually head for the clothes, shoes, jewelry, books, and galley accessory booths, while my captain deliberates over boring things like metal fittings, engines, and electronic devices.

Boat shows are a good place to pick up catalogs and brochures to bring home and add to your winter reading pile. You can usually order items you saw at a boat show at boat show prices for several weeks afterwards, so don't think you got off cheap just because you left without making a major purchase. During long winters, perusing through catalogs is another good way to keep the summer alive.

An increasing trend at boat shows is to offer seminars and demonstrations on various aspects of boating. You will want to attend some of these; your captain will want to attend all of them. We attend many of the shows in the Northeast that are a comfortable day's drive from our home, but we also like to make a vacation around a show. In the past few years, we have enjoyed jaunts to Maryland over the Columbus Day weekend to visit the huge in-the-water show in Annapolis, and to New Jersey for the late January-early February SailExpo in Atlantic City. We've fought ice and snowstorms to make the Atlantic City show! We haven't gotten to the Miami show in March yet, but I hear it is spectacular.

Boat Show Attire

Don't forget that, when you go to a boat show, you will be climbing on and off boats. Therefore, dress appropriately. You will not be allowed on a boat unless you are wearing boat shoes or rubber-soled shoes. (Sneakers or flats with rubber soles are fine.) On some of the more prestigious boats, you'll be asked to remove your shoes regardless of what kind you are wearing, so wear a shoe style that you can slip on and off easily. If you are shoeless on a boat, be careful of slipping, especially if you are wearing nylons. Cotton socks are a bit less slippery. I think that going barefoot on show boats during the winter is tacky, but I have no qualms about doing so in the summer (as long as my toenails are painted!).

A boat show is a perfect occasion to wear nautical sweaters, sailboat earrings, crisp white or navy pants or shorts, stylish boat shoes, or anything with your boat's name on it. Doing so will separate you from the tourists and gain you the serious attention of the vendors.

PLANNING A WINTER CHARTER VACATION

After you have a few boating seasons behind you, you probably will have developed the skills that are necessary to captain your own boat in a lovely foreign port. If you've never chartered a bareboat before, and don't feel you are ready to manage the responsibility, you can always hire a captain (and a cook). Imagine going someplace on a boat, where the weather is ideal and the beauty is mind-boggling. Then, ice the cake with a good dollop of privacy because even in high season many spots are not crowded. Unlike vacationing at a resort or a fancy hotel, you can wear what you want, go when and where you wish, and enjoy a choice of native dishes or fancy cuisine.

We have chartered boats in the Caribbean, the Grenadines, Grenada, St. Martin, and our all-time favorite, Tahiti. Just think what fun it would be to brag that you've not only traveled to these places, but you've sailed the waters there. Charter companies are located in almost every exotic sailing area you can think of.

I have two pieces of advice if you are a novice at chartering.

Use a major charter company. They are most informative about traveling in local waters and their boats are always clean and in good repair. If your dinghy engine or refrigerators breaks, you can get speedy assistance because they have support bases in place throughout the cruising area.

My other caution is more personal. Pick your crew carefully. A charter trip can make or break friendships. The people you travel with don't necessarily need to be experienced boaters, but they should be flexible, fun loving, easy to be around, and not prone to seasickness.

See, I Told You So

I told you it would come down to this. You're a sailor! We share something very special—the joy of sailing. Sailing to ports unknown, exploring remote anchorages, and docking at fancy marinas. We have it all, we have choices. We travel on our own schedules, at our own pace, and do the things we truly enjoy. Maybe we'll fish, maybe we'll swim. Maybe we'll just lounge in the cockpit with a good book. It doesn't matter what we do as long as we are here on our boat, because we *love* it!

APPENDIX

A partial list of marine stores (with branches all over the country) and catalogs

Boat US 1-800-937-2628   Welcome Aboard 1-800-295-2469
West Marine 1-800-262-8464   M&E Marine 1-800-541-6501
Defender 1-800-628-8225

Other good sources for boating apparel and accessories:
Eddie Bauer 1-800-426-8020 www.eddiebauer.com
Lands' End 1-800-356-4444 www.landsend.com
L.L. Bean 1-800-221-4221 www.llbean.com

WHERE TO FIND
Long-lasting canvas tote bags:
Custom Canvas, Thames Street, Newport, RI. 401-847-4977
Good quality soft coolers:
Horizons Ltd., Conyers, GA. 1-800-969-4583
Special mattresses:
For a custom coil mattress for any shape berth, contact Handcraft Mattress Company, Santa Ana, CA. 1-800-241-7751
Select Comfort offers air mattresses (with adjustable levels of firmness) for queen, center cockpit aft berths. 1-800-344-6561
A water filter that works:
Seagull IV X-1FP built-in water filter by General Ecology, 151 Sheree Boulevard, Exton, PA 19341   1-800-441-8166; fax: 610-363- 0412
Tasty multifunction sauces:
Otwell Specialty Foods, Hartford, CT; High Seas Collection; 860-523-7647; fax: 860-232-8411
Good sunscreen:
Bull Frog. Also, Nauticare Naturals makes a sun care line specifically for mariners; 1-800-262-0202
Protective clothing:
The Sunbrella clothing line is designed to act like a 30+ SPF sunscreen. Some catalogs that feature Sunbrella and other brands of protective outerwear are: Precautions: 1-800-882-7860, and Travel Smith Outfitting Guide and Catalog: 1-800-950-1600
Saltwater shampoo:
We've always used Vidal Sassoon products, but Sea Savon and other products are also formulated to suds and clean in salt water.

Basic boating classes:
The United States Power Squadron offers classes in piloting and small-boat handling, in which students learn nautical terms, boat safety, and basic piloting. Call 1-888-FOR-USPS (1-888-367-8777), or check out their website: www.usps.org for more information.

On-board boating instruction:
Annapolis Sailing School
601 6th Street, Annapolis, MD 21403   1-800-638-9192 website: www. usboat.com/annapway/
Steve and Doris Colgate's Offshore Sailing School
16731 McGregor Boulevard, Ft. Meyers, FL 33908   941-454-1191; website: www.offshore@coco.net

Organizations for women in boating
National Women's Sailing Association, 16731 McGregor Boulevard, Ft. Meyers, FL 33908; 1-800-566-NWSA
Womenship Waves, Sailing School for Women; 1-800-342-9295; fax: 410-263-2036
Sea Sense; 1-800-332-1404

Magazines and Newpapers to peruse
Cruising World, cruising magazine for worldwide sailors
Latitudes & Attitudes, cruising magazine for sailors with a sense of humor
Long Island Boating World, a free newpaper for Connecticut and Long Island boaters
Motorboating & Sailing, good basic boating magazine with some practical boatkeeping tips
Northeast Sailing Life, harbor and marina information for Northeast coastal sailors
Practical Sailor, nonbiased consumer's guide to products used by sailors
SAIL, popular cruising magazine
Sailing, large photos. Focus on the Great Lakes
Soundings, news and classified
The Ensign, the official magazine of the U.S. Power Squadron (you get it free when you join). I find a wealth of boatkeeping tips in it.
Yachting, a magazine for those with *big* boats, power and sail.
There are many more and new ones are always coming out. A magazine exists for every facet of boating. Look for them in the magazine sections in bookstores and at marine stores. Complimentary sample copies are often available at boat shows. Also, check out the websites for these magazines; many offer special services and interactive chats.

Books for boaters: These are the bibles of boating. If you don't have them, get them.
Chapman Piloting, Seamanship, and Small Boat Handling, Elbert Maloney, ed. Hearst Marine Books, NY
The Annapolis Book of Seamanship, John Rousmaniere. Simon and Schuster, NY
Every boater should have a current version of the following publications aboard for anticipated cruising areas:

A waterway guide for each area, such as *Embassy's Complete Boating Guide and Chartbook*
Reed's Nautical Almanac, Thomas Reed Publications, Inc., Boston, MA (website:www.ReedsAlmanac.com)
Up-to-date navigation charts
Eldridge Tide & Pilot Book, Marion Jeuid White and Robert Eldridge White, Jr. Boston, MA

The following books are geared to the offshore sailor, yet there is a wealth of information in them for women who are recreational boaters:
The Cruising Woman's Advisor, Diane Jessie. International Marine, Camden, ME
How to Live Aboard a Boat, Janet Groene. Hearst Marine Books, New York, NY
Cooking on the Go, Janet Groene. Hearst Marine Books, New York, NY
There are numerous other cookbooks and provisioning guides to help you spend more (or less) time in the galley

Two of the largest sources of nautical books
The Armchair Sailor, 543 Thames Street, Newport, RI 02840 1-800-29CHART
Website: www.seabooks.com
Bluewater Books and Charts, 141 SE 17th Street, Ft. Lauderdale, FL 1-800-942-258
Website: www.Bluewaterweb.com
Wherever you sail, check out local libraries, bookstores, and marine stores for nautical books

The major publishers of nautical books
Sheridan House Inc. To order a catalog, call toll-free 1-888-SHERIBK, or visit their website at www.sheridanhouse.com
International Marine. To order a catalog, call toll-free 1-800-262-4729.

Index